Bond Markets
Structures and Yield Calculations

◆ Patrick J. Brown ◆

Glenlake Publishing Company, Ltd.
Chicago • London • New Delhi

Fitzroy Dearborn Publishers
Chicago and London

© 1998 International Securities Market Association

ISBN: 1-888998-55-5

Library edition: Fitzroy Dearborn Publishers, Chicago and London
ISBN:

All rights reserved. No part of this book may be reproduced in any form or by any means, electronic, mechanical photocopying, recording, or otherwise without the prior written permission of the publisher.

Printed in the United States of America.

GPCo
1261 West Glenlake
Chicago, Illinois 60660
glenlake@ix.netcom.com
www.glenlake.com

CONTENTS

Preface v

Acknowledgements vi

Chapter 1 **Introduction** 1

Chapter 2 **Trade, Value and Settlement Dates** 2

Chapter 3 **Accrued Interest** 5
    3.1 Counting days accrued 5
    3.2 Days in the year 9
    3.3. Accrued interest computation 12

Chapter 4 **Measures of Life and Associated Calculations** 13
    4.1 Life to maturity 14
    4.2 Life to next call 14
    4.3 Life to put 15
    4.4 Average life 15
    4.5 Equivalent life 16
    4.6 Duration 17
    4.7 Modified duration or volatility 20
    4.8 Convexity 21

Chapter 5 **Yields** 23
    5.1 Current yield 23
    5.2 Simple yield to maturity 24
    5.3 Redemption yields 25
        5.3.1 Fixed coupon bonds 27
        5.3.2 Money market yields 30
            (bonds in their last coupon period)
        5.3.3 Zero coupon bonds 33
        5.3.4 Undated securities 34

Contents

	5.3.5	Bonds with sinking funds (yields to average/equivalent life)	35
	5.3.6	Other bond types	37
	5.3.7	Other redemption yields	38

Chapter 6 **Floating Rate Note Calculations** 40
    6.1 Simple margin 40
    6.2 Discounted margin 42
    6.3 Yields 44

Chapter 7 **Convertible Calculations** 47
    7.1 Conversion premium/discount - ratio 47
    7.2 Income differential and break-even period 49

Chapter 8 **Warrants** 51
    8.1 Bond warrants 51
    8.2 Equity warrants 53
    8.3 Commodity/currency warrants 54

Chapter 9 **Money Market Instruments** 56
    9.1 Discounts 56
    9.2 Yields 58
        9.2.1 With one coupon payment 58
        9.2.2 With more than one coupon payment 59
    9.3 Floating rate certificates of deposit 60

Chapter 10 **Miscellaneous** 61
    10.1 Bonds in default 61
    10.2 Tax 61
    10.3 Prices from yields 62

Chapter 11 **Bond Market Comparisons** 65
    11.1 Table headings 72
    11.2 Footnotes 76

Appendix I
    The General Redemption Yield Formula 89

Appendix II
    Compounding Frequency Adjustments 92

Appendix III
    Index-Linked Stocks and Real Returns 94

PREFACE

The increase in cross market bond trading, makes it very important that participants understand the differences between market practices and as a result can compare returns on a consistent basis.

Due, at least in part, to the G30 recommendations, the advent of the Euro and increased cross-border investment, bond market practices and yield conventions are tending to converge. However, it can be seen that there is still a long way to go.

The purpose of this book is to define and compare the standard methods and conventions used in the International and many domestic bond markets for calculating prices, accrued interest, yields, durations etc. The comparison concentrates on the European bond markets, but it does include some of the other major markets.

The book incorporates, updates and extends the information contained in the ISMA Formulae for Yield and Other Calculations book (now out of print) and that in the Bond Markets Mechanics chapter of the 6th Edition of the European Bond Markets book.

Patrick Brown
London

ACKNOWLEDGEMENTS

I would like to thank the members of the EFFAS European Bond Commission, their national bond societies and numerous other people, without whom the chapter on bond market comparisons would not have been possible.

David Self of the International Securities Market Association has given me invaluable help in the compilation of the book for which I am most grateful. I would also like to thank my secretary, Diane Dowie, who has handled a most difficult task with great skill and patience.

CHAPTER 1

INTRODUCTION

The bond markets in Europe and elsewhere have developed independently with inevitably different conventions for calculating prices, yields and interest rates and settling the various instruments. With the ever increasing amount of cross-border trading it is desirable that people should be able to compare accurately the markets in one country with another and agree the cost of the transactions. The purpose of this book is to help in the process.

The practices of the individual markets are constantly changing and these changes are tending to make the markets more homogeneous - partly due to the influence of the G30 recommendations, but more significantly, due to the greatly increased amount of cross-border trading and the advent of the euro.

Examples of this are the wide acceptance of the ISMA yield methodology, which is included in the Maastricht treaty, and the standard money market yield calculation. Similarly, there has been a move to settling bond transactions internationally, in many European domestic markets and in the U.S. corporate market on a T+3 basis (i.e. 3 business days after trade date).

However, the different bond and money markets still continue to accrue interest on a variety of bases, to trade ex-coupon for different periods etc. For example, currently in France, the money markets accrue interest on a 360-day year basis, whereas the bond markets accrue on a 365/366-day year. The situation is reversed in Italy, with the money markets accruing interest on a 365-day year and the bond markets on a 360-day year.

It should be noted that, whilst every effort has been made to establish the validity of the data, the constantly changing nature of the markets inevitably creates a potential for errors and omissions, for which neither the author or publisher can accept liability.

CHAPTER 2

TRADE, VALUE AND SETTLEMENT DATES

Most markets have rules for determining the value date of a transaction. For example, the value date for a transaction in an applicable international security is governed by ISMA Rules 221-225. The rules as at January 1997 are given below:

Rule 221 Value date new issues

The value date for a transaction effected prior to the closing date shall be the closing date or the third business day following the trade date, whichever is the later.

A business day for the purpose of this rule shall be a day when Cedel, Euroclear and the cash market of the currency in which the relevant transaction is to be settled are open for business.

In case either Cedel, Euroclear or the cash market of the currency in which the relevant transaction is to be settled, are closed for business between the trade date and the value date, accrued interest shall be adjusted.

Rule 222 Normal value date

The value date for a transaction effected on or after the closing date shall be the third business day (as defined in rule 221) following the trade date.

In case either Cedel, Euroclear or the cash market of the currency in which the relevant transaction is to be settled, are closed for business between the trade date and the value date, accrued interest shall be adjusted.

Trade, Value and Settlement Dates

Rule 223 Special value date

A special value date may be mutually agreed between the buyer and the seller at the time of dealing.

Rule 224 Value date on non-settlement day

Deleted effective June 1, 1995.

Rule 225 Value date and coupon due date

Where the due date of an interest coupon coincides with the value date of a transaction, the buyer shall not acquire such coupon and no accrued interest shall be calculated on such a contract. With the exception of floating rate notes, in the case of a transaction with a value date on the thirtieth calendar day and a coupon due date on the thirty-first calendar day of the same month, accrued interest shall correspond to the full value of the coupon.

The value date and the settlement date are normally identical. It is conventional and recommended that all calculations on securities are performed to the value date and not the settlement date if there is a discrepancy.

Similarly if a coupon or redemption falls on a non-settlement date then all calculations are performed as if the payment were to be made on that date.

The worst problem that can arise is when a bond is expected to be redeemed on a non-settlement date e.g. Taylor Woodrow 8 ¾% 1 December 1990 which was redeemed on a Saturday. The terms of most new international issues are now chosen so that this does not occur, however in some domestic markets, e.g. the Netherlands and Germany, it is a common occurrence, because of their coupon payment conventions.

Example ▶

If the cost of overnight money is 10% then the cost of a two day delay on the redemption payment is $10 \times 2/365 = 0.0548\%$.

Coupons on fixed rate bonds will frequently occur at weekends and on bank holidays. However, this should not happen with floating rate notes as the issuing houses normally follow the convention below.

The interest payment date is the date falling six calendar months after the closing date and each date thereafter which falls six calendar months after the preceding interest payment date. If any interest payment date would otherwise fall on a day which is not a business day, it shall be postponed to the next business day unless it would thereby fall in the next calendar month. In the latter event, the interest payment date shall be the immediately preceding business day, and each subsequent interest payment date

BOND MARKETS: STRUCTURES AND YIELD CALCULATIONS

shall be the last business day of the sixth calendar month after the month in which the preceding interest payment date shall have fallen.

Example ▸

Consider a floating rate note which pays a monthly coupon on Tuesday, 28 January 1996. The subsequent coupon payment dates will be:

28 February	*Friday*
30 March	*Monday*
30 April	*Thursday*
29 May	*Friday*
30 June	*Tuesday*
31 July	*Friday*
28 August	*Friday (assuming 31 August is not a business day)*
30 September	*Wednesday*

CHAPTER 3

ACCRUED INTEREST

The prices of bonds in most markets are normally quoted 'Clean', i.e. without any accrued interest, which has to be paid by the purchaser. However, there are occasions when the trade is agreed on a 'Flat' or Gross' price, i.e. without any accrued adjustment. This sometimes occurs because the payment of interest is uncertain, e.g. the issuer is in default and it is not clear if the accrued interest will ever be received. It also occurs with repo transactions where the convention in the market is to agree a 'Flat' price for the collateral. On the other hand buy/sell back transactions tend to follow the normal bond market conventions.

Accrual basis

Securities accrue interest in a variety of ways, according to the number of days since issue or the last coupon date. In the majority of cases the accrued interest which has to be added to the price is equal to:

assumed rate of interest × *number of days accrued / number of days in the year.*

There are several methods of counting the number of days accrued and in the year. They are described below.

3.1. Counting Days Accrued

There are basically three methods of counting the number of days accrued interest, although they are subject to variation:

- Actual calendar days, including 29 February if it occurs in the period.
- 30-day month European Method
- 30-day month U.S. Method

For international securities, ISMA rule 251 specifies how accrued interest should be calculated for fixed and floating rate securities. Fixed rate securities currently follow the 30-day month European method, whereas floating rate notes use actual days.

BOND MARKETS: STRUCTURES AND YIELD CALCULATIONS

However, it is expected that all international securities issued after 31 December 1998 will use actual calendar days for the calculation of accrued interest. ISMA rule 251 (January 1997) specifies:

Rule 251 Accrued interest calculation

251.1 *With the exception of floating rate notes, accrued interest on a contract shall be calculated on a 360-days per year basis (each calendar month to be considered one-twelfth of 360-days, or thirty days, and each period from a date in one month to the same date in the following month to be considered thirty days) from and including the date of the last paid interest coupon or the day from which interest is to accrue for a new issue, up to but excluding the value date of the transaction.*

Examples of calculations in conformity with Rules 225 (see chapter 2) and 251:

Interest accrues from coupon dates	Value dates	Number of days of accrued interest for straight and convertible bonds	floating rate notes normal	leap year
	the following year:		normal	leap year
30.11.	28.2.	88	90	90
30.11.	29.2.	89		91
30.11.	1.3.	91	91	92
30.11.	3.3.	93	93	94
30.11.	30.3.	120	120	121
30.11.	31.3.	120	121	122
31.12.	28.2.	58	59	59
31.12.	29.2.	59		60
31.12.	1.3.	61	60	61
31.12.	3.3.	63	62	63
31.12.	30.3.	90	89	90
31.12.	31.3.	90	90	91
	the same year:			
1.1.	28.2.	57	58	58
1.1.	29.2.	58		59
1.1.	1.3.	60	59	60
1.1.	3.3.	62	61	62
1.1.	30.3.	89	88	89
1.1.	31.3.	89	89	90
15.1.	28.2.	43	44	44
15.1.	29.2.	44		45
15.1.	1.3.	46	45	46
15.1.	3.3.	48	47	48
1.2.	28.2.	27	27	27
1.2.	29.2.	28		28
1.2.	1.3.	30	28	29
1.2.	3.3.	32	30	31

ACCRUED INTEREST

Interest accrues from coupon dates	Value dates	Number of days of accrued interest for straight and convertible bonds		floating rate notes
15.2.	28.2.	13	13	13
15.2.	29.2.	14		14
15.2.	1.3.	16	14	15
15.2.	3.3.	18	16	17
28.2.	29.2.	1		1
28.2.	1.3.	3	1	2
28.2.	3.3.	5	3	4
28.2.	5.3.	7	5	6
28.2.	30.3.	32	30	31
28.2.	31.3.	32	31	32
	the following year:			
28.2.	27.2.	359	364	365
28.2.	28.2.	0*	0*	0*

* seller collects full interest coupon, no accrued interest calculation to the buyer.

251.2 With the exception of floating rate notes, accrued interest to a value date on the thirty-first calendar day of a month shall be the same as to the thirtieth calendar day of the same month.

251.3 Accrued interest on a contract for floating rate notes shall be calculated on actual days, divided by 360 (or by 365 in the case of a Euro-sterling issue) from and including the date of the last paid interest coupon or the day from which interest is to accrue for a new issue, up to but excluding the value date of the transaction.

251.4 No accrued interest shall be calculated where rule 225 (see chapter 2) applies or where the value date coincides with the date of issue or where a transaction has been concluded at a 'flat' price.

Rule 251.3 above states that the accrued interest on Euro-sterling floating rate notes is calculated by dividing the actual days accrued by 365 and multiplying by the coupon rate. This is always true for bonds where the next coupon payment is in a non-leap year, but for coupon payments in a leap year the actual number of days is normally divided by 366. However, there are a few Euro-sterling issues where the issue documentation, which should be followed, specifies that the number of days accrued has to be divided by 365 even in a leap year.

As can be seen, in the European 30-day method (30E) the 31st of a month is always counted as if it were the 30th, and there are three days from 28 February to 1 March, even in a leap year.

In other words, if the interest accrues from date $D_1/M_1/Y_1$ to a value date of $D_2/M_2/Y_2$, then the number of days accrued can be calculated as follows:

7

If $D_1 = 31$, set it to 30

If $D_2 = 31$, set it to 30

Number of days accrued = $(D_2 - D_1) + 30 \times (M_2 - M_1) + 360 \times (Y_2 - Y_1)$

In the U.S. method (30U), the 31st of a month is counted - unless the period being measured is from the 30th or 31st of a previous month, when the period is counted as a whole number of months (i.e. it is a multiple of 30).

In this case, if the interest accrues from date $D_1/M_1/Y_1$ to a value date of $D_2/M_2/Y_2$, then the number of days accrued can be calculated as follows:

If $D_1 = 31$, set it to 30

If $D_2 = 31$ and D_1 is 30 or 31 set D_2 to 30, otherwise leave as 31.

Number of days accrued = $(D_2 - D_1) + 30 \times (M_2 - M_1) + 360 \times (Y_2 - Y_1)$

In the U.S. method if a bond has a coupon date on the last day of February it is treated as if it were on the 30th February.

Example ▶

Consider a bond which follows the U.S. method with semi-annual coupon payments maturing on 31 August 2005. The other coupon payment is normally the last day of February. The number of days accrued interest is on the following dates.

	Days accrued		Days accrued
27 February 1996	177	27 February 1997	177
28 February 1996	178	28 February 1997	0
29 February 1996	0		
1 March 1996	1	1 March 1997	1
30 August 1996	180	30 August 1997	180
31 August 1996	0	31 August 1997	0

The following figure shows a comparison of some of the differences between the ISMA/European, the U.S. and the actual methods of calculating the number of days accrued.

		No. of days between Date 1 & Date 2		
Date 1	Date 2	ISMA Method	U.S. Method	Actual
29 July	31 August	31	32	33
30 July	31 August	30	30	32
31 July	31 August	30	30	31

ACCRUED INTEREST

1 August	31 August	29	30	30
29 July	1 September	32	32	34
30 July	1 September	31	31	33
31 July	1 September	31	31	32
1 August	1 September	30	30	31

3.2 Days in the Year

There are four main ways of determining the number of days in the year. They are: 360, 365, actual days in the year (i.e. 365 unless it is a leap year when it is 366), and actual days in the coupon period multiplied by the number of coupon periods in a year.

The number of days in the year is not dependent on the method of calculating the number of days accrued. (For example, in the floating rate note Euromarket, for all currencies other than sterling and the Irish pound, the accrued is based on actual days since the issue or last coupon date divided by 360. In other words a floating rate note held for one year will produce an income greater than the average quoted coupon. Floating rate sterling and Irish pound notes use a 365-day year).

If the year is deemed to be actual days and allows for leap years (365/366), the convention in the Eurobond market is to divide by 366 for all coupon payments which occur in a leap year, unless there is only one payment per year. In this latter case, the payment period which includes 29 February is divided by 366. On the other hand, in the French market, the convention is to divide by 366 if a leap day occurs in the calendar year before the coupon date.

Example ▸

If a bond which accrues on a 365/366-day year has normal coupon dates of 15 January and 15 July, then the number of days in the year for each coupon period will be:

Coupon Period			Eurobond	French bond
15 January 1995	-	15 July 1995	365-day year	365-day year
15 July 1995	-	15 January 1996	366-day year	365-day year
15 January 1996	-	15 July 1996	366-day year	366-day year
15 July 1996	-	15 January 1997	365-day year	366-day year

On the other hand, if the bond only had one payment on 15 January, the calculation would be:

Coupon Period			
15 January 1995	-	15 January 1996	365-day year
15 January 1996	-	15 January 1997	366-day year

BOND MARKETS: STRUCTURES AND YIELD CALCULATIONS

The position with leap years is further complicated by the 1991 International Swaps and Derivatives Association (ISDA) definitions for "day count fraction". This is specified as the method to follow in some medium-term note programmes.

The 1991 ISDA definition states:

"Day count fraction" means, in respect of a swap transaction and the calculation of a fixed amount, a floating amount, a compounding period amount or an FRA amount,

a) if "actual/365" or "actual/actual" is specified, the actual number of days in the calculation period or compounding period in respect of which payment is being made divided by 365 (or, if any portion of that calculation period or compounding period falls in a leap year, the sum of (A) the actual number of days in that portion of the calculation period or compounding period falling in a leap year divided by 366 and (B) the actual number of days in that portion of the calculation period or compounding period falling in a non-leap year divided by 365);

b) if "actual/365 (fixed)" is specified, the actual number of days in the calculation period or compounding period in respect of which payment is being made divided by 365;

ISDA are in the process of reviewing their definitions.

For the purpose of accruing interest some markets define the number of days in a year to be the actual days in the coupon period times the number of periods per annum. Markets which use this method include the U.S. Treasury market, and the proposed U.K. gilt-edged and international fixed-rate bond markets.

Example ▸

A U.S. Treasury bond with an 8% coupon in a 184 day 6-month period accrues interest at a daily rate of:

$$8 / (2 \times 184) = 0.021739\%$$

Similarly in a 181 day 6-month period it accrues interest at a daily rate of:

$$8 / (2 \times 181) = 0.022099\%$$

Some bonds are issued with 'short' or 'long' first coupon periods. For these, a theoretical number of days in the period(s) has to be calculated.

The first coupon period is deemed to start on what would have been the normal coupon date on or before the date interest starts accruing on the bond.

ACCRUED INTEREST

If the date interest starts accruing is before what would have been the coupon date prior to the first coupon date, then the period has to be split into two quasi interest periods for the calculation.

Example ▶

For bonds with an 8% coupon issued on 1 February 1999 (with interest accruing from this date).

Coupon Payment Date(s)	First Coupon Payment Date	First Coupon Period Days in Year Calculation	Daily Accrual Rate	First Coupon Payment
1 Feb	1 Feb 2000	1 Feb 1999-1 Feb 2000 (365 days)	8/365	8%
1 July	1 July 1999	1 July 1998-1 July 1999 (365 days)	8/365	8 × 150/365% (1 Feb-1 July = 150 days)
1 July	1 July 2000	1 July 1998-1 July 2000 (731 days split into 2 periods)		Note 1
	Period 1	1 July 1998-1 July 1999 (365 days)	8/365	
	Period 2	1 July 1999-1 July 2000 (366 days)	8/366	
1 Feb, Aug	1 Aug 1999	1 Feb 1999-1 Aug 1999 (181 days)	8/(2 × 181)	4%
1 Jan, July	1 July 1999	1 Jan 1999-1 July 1999 (181 days)	8/(2 × 181)	8 × 150/362% (1Feb-1 July = 150 days)
1 Jan, July	1 Jan 2000	1 Jan 1999-1 Jan 2000 (365 days split into 2 periods)		Note 2
	Period 1	1 Jan 1999-1 July 1999 (181 days)	8/(2 × 181)	
	Period 2	1 July 1999-1 Jan 2000 (184 days)	8/(2 × 184)	

Note 1   The first coupon payment is: $8 \times 150/365 + 8 \times 366/366$% as there are 150 days from 1 February 1999 to 1 July 1999

Note 2   The first coupon payment is: $8 \times 150/(2 \times 181) + 8 \times 184/(2 \times 184)$% as there are 150 days from 1 February 1999 to 1 July 1999.

BOND MARKETS: STRUCTURES AND YIELD CALCULATIONS

It can be seen that for a bond which pays an annual coupon, this method is equivalent to the actual days in the year method.

In most markets interest accrues from the issue date or last coupon date (inclusive) to the settlement date (exclusive), however this is not universally true. For example, in Italy, both the coupon and settlement dates are counted.

3.3. Accrued interest computation

For international bonds, ISMA Rule 252 below specifies the method of rounding U.S. dollar accrued interest.

Rule 252 Accrued interest computation - fractions

In all transactions involving the payment of interest, fractions of a cent equalling or exceeding 5 mills shall be regarded as one cent and fractions of a cent less than 5 mills shall be disregarded. Examples:

$ 137.625 accrued interest has to be increased to $ 137.63.
$ 137.624 accrued interest has to be decreased to $ 137.62.

For other currencies accrued interest should be rounded to the nearest convenient currency unit in a similar way.

CHAPTER 4

MEASURES OF LIFE AND ASSOCIATED CALCULATIONS

It has been seen that currently international straight bonds accrue interest on the basis of twelve 30 day months (i.e. 360-days in a year), whereas international floating-rate notes accrue interest on every calendar day. When calculating the life or other time measure of a security, the various conventions are continued, although they result in slightly different results.

For any international non-floating rate security including warrants, the period between two dates $D_1/M_1/Y_1$ and $D_2/M_2/Y_2$ is given in days by:

If $D_1 = 31$, set $D_1 = 30$.

If $D_2 = 31$, set $D_2 = 30$.

Number of days = $(D_2 - D_1) + 30 \times (M_2 - M_1) + 360 \times (Y_2 - Y_1)$

For floating-rate notes the period between two dates in years is the number of complete years moving forward from the first date plus the actual number of days for the fractional period at the end divided by 365 or 366 if the fractional period includes 29 February.

Example ▶

The period from 1 February 1998 to 1 August 2000 is considered to be a two year period from 1 February 1998 to 1 February 2000 plus a part period from 1 February 2000 to 1 August 2000. The part period being 182 days = 182/366 years = 0.497 years. Thus the total period is 2.497 years.

Bond Markets: Structures and Yield Calculations

If the whole years are calculated back from the last date, a different answer is obtained, as the part period is now from 1 February 1998 to 1 August 1998 which is only 181 days.

Examples of the calculations using international bonds are given below:

Date 1	Date 2	Type of security	Period in years and days		Period in years
1 August 1993	1 February 1994	straight	0 years	180 days	0.500
1 August 1993	1 February 1994	FRN	0 years	184 days	0.504
1 February 1994	1 August 1995	straight	1 year	180 days	1.500
1 February 1994	1 August 1995	FRN	1 year	181 days	1.496
1 February 1994	1 August 1996	straight	2 years	180 days	2.500
1 February 1994	1 August 1996	FRN	2 years	182 days	2.497*
1 January 1994	31 December 1994	straight	0 years	359 days	0.997
1 January 1994	31 December 1994	FRN	0 years	364 days	0.997
1 January 1996	31 December 1996	Straight	0 years	359 days	0.997
1 January 1996	31 December 1996	FRN	0 years	365 days	0.997*

* *The fractional periods are part of 366-day years.*

Various measures of life are applied to securities. They include life to maturity, next call, put, extension period, average life, equivalent life and duration. Lives are always measured from the value date to the assumed redemption date(s) using the appropriate calendar convention.

4.1 Life to maturity

The maturity date of a bond is assumed to be the final normal maturity date. Any extendible or retractable dates are ignored.

4.2 Life to next call

Bonds are often callable by the issuer prior to maturity upon a set notice period, e.g. they may be callable only on coupon dates, at annual intervals, or at any time during the call period.

Example ▸

Consider the following variations of a bond which has an 8% coupon payable semi-annually on 1 January and 1 July, and a final redemption date on 1 July 1998 provided it has not been previously called. It may be called on 30 days notice between 1 January 1993 and 30 June 1996 at:

    either a)   any time
    or   b)   on a coupon date
    or   c)   annually on 1 July

MEASURES OF LIFE AND ASSOCIATED CALCULATIONS

Trade date	Earliest next call dates		
	Option (a)	Option (b)	Option (c)
1 January 1990	1 January 1993	1 January 1993	1 July 1993
1 December 1992	1 January 1993	1 January 1993	1 July 1993
2 December 1992	2 January 1993	1 July 1993	1 July 1993
1 June 1993	1 July 1993	1 July 1993	1 July 1993
2 June 1993	2 July 1993	1 January 1994	1 July 1994
2 June 1995	2 July 1995	1 January 1996	Not callable
2 December 1995	2 January 1996	Not callable	Not callable
1 June 1996	Not callable	Not callable	Not callable

4.3 Life to put

It is conventional to calculate the life to put to the next put opportunity.

4.4. Average life

The average life of a bond is the period from the value date to the average of the future sinking fund dates weighted by the non-discounted repayments.

Some bonds have purchase funds, which enable stock to be purchased in the market within specified price ranges. Purchase funds are not mandatory and hence do not affect the long term return of an investor and so are ignored in the calculation of average life.

The average life is given by:

$$AL = \frac{\sum_{i=1}^{n} A_i \cdot L_i}{\sum_{i=1}^{n} A_i} \qquad (4.1)$$

where:
- AL = average life
- n = number of future capital repayments
- A_i = ith future repayment amount
- L_i = time in years to the ith repayment

Example ▶

If a bond has a sinking fund of:

20% to be redeemed on 1 June 1999
10% to be redeemed on 1 June 2000
70% to be redeemed on 1 June 2001

BOND MARKETS: STRUCTURES AND YIELD CALCULATIONS

then the average life on 1 June 1994 can be calculated as follows:

$$\text{Average life} = \frac{20 \times 5 + 10 \times 6 + 70 \times 7}{20 + 10 + 70} = 6.5 \text{ years}$$

i.e. the average redemption date is 1 December 2000.

It can be seen that the average life of a security continuously decreases over time between repayments, but jumps on a repayment date.

4.5 Equivalent life

The concept of equivalent life is very similar to that of average life for bonds with sinking funds, except that now the capital repayments are discounted at the redemption yield rate.

The equivalent life of a bond is the period from the value date to the average of the future sinking fund dates weighted by the discounted capital repayments. This means that the equivalent life is slightly shorter than the average life.

The equivalent life is given by:

$$EL = \frac{\sum_{i=1}^{n} A_i \cdot L_i \cdot v^{L_i}}{\sum_{i=1}^{n} A_i \cdot v^{L_i}} \qquad (4.2)$$

where:
- EL = equivalent life
- n = number of future capital repayments
- A_i = ith future repayment amount
- L_i = time in years to the ith repayment
- v = annualized discounting factor
  i.e. if the annualized yield is y then $v = 1/(1 + y)$
  ($y = 0.08$ for a yield of 8%)

Example ▸

Using the same example as in average life of a bond which is redeemed at par in three instalments, such that 20% is redeemed on 1 June 1999, 10% on 1 June 2000 and 70% on 1 June 2001. Assuming the bond has an annualized redemption yield allowing for this schedule of 10% then the equivalent life on 1 June 1994 is given by:

$$v = 1/(1 + 0.1) = 0.90909$$

$$EL = \frac{20 \times 5v^5 + 10 \times 6v^6 + 70 \times 7v^7}{20 \times v^5 + 10 \times v^6 + 70 \times v^7}$$

Measures of Life and Associated Calculations

$$= \frac{62.092 + 33.868 + 251.447}{12.418 + 5.645 + 35.921}$$

$$= 6.435 \text{ years}$$

4.6. Duration

The concept of life to maturity, average or equivalent life does not give the investor a true indication of the life of a bond, since it does not take into account any coupon payments. There is, for example, a lot of difference from an investment point of view between a zero coupon 10 year bond and an 11% 10 year bond, since the former only makes one payment after 10 years while the latter pays coupons during its life of more than its redemption value.

The concept of duration is a better measure of the life of the investment, as it takes into account both the coupon and the redemption payments. Duration is defined to be the average life of the present values of all future cash flows from the bond. In calculating the present value of the future cash flows a discount rate equal to the redemption yield of the bond is used.

Mathematically duration is given by:

$$D = \frac{\sum_{i=1}^{n} CF_i \cdot L_i \cdot v^{L_i}}{\sum_{i=1}^{n} CF_i \cdot v^{L_i}} \quad (4.3)$$

where: D = duration
n = number of future coupon and capital cash flows
CF_i = ith future cash flow
L_i = time in years to the ith cash flow
v = annualized discounting factor
i.e. if the annualized yield is y then $v = 1/(1 + y)$
($y = 0.08$ for a yield of 8%)

Since the gross price of a bond is just the present value of all future cash flows equation (4.3) can be re-written:

$$D = \frac{1}{P} \cdot \sum_{i=1}^{n} CF_i \cdot L_i \cdot v^{L_i} \quad (4.4)$$

where: P = gross price (i.e. clean price plus accrued interest).

The above calculations are also known as the Macaulay Duration.

BOND MARKETS: STRUCTURES AND YIELD CALCULATIONS

For a zero coupon bond the duration is the same as the life to maturity.

For a bond with a fixed coupon g payable h times per annum, with a normal first coupon payment, which is redeemable on one coupon date, it can be shown that the duration can be given by:

$$D = \frac{f1}{h} + \frac{g \cdot v^{f1}}{P \cdot h^2} \cdot \left\{ v + 2v^2 + \cdots + (n-1)v^{n-1} \right\} + \frac{C}{P \cdot h} \cdot (n-1)v^{n+f1-1} \quad (4.5)$$

where: D = duration
g = annual coupon rate %
h = number of coupon payments per year
n = number of coupon payments to redemption
P = gross price (i.e. clean price plus accrued interest)
C = redemption value
$f1$ = fraction of a period from value date to the first interest payment date. A period is defined as the normal time between two consecutive coupon payments
v = discounting factor i.e. if the yield compounded h times per annum is y then $v = 1/(1 + y/h)$
($y = 0.08$ for a yield of 8%)

Example ▶

Consider the following bond which pays an annual 9% coupon, is trading at par and is redeemed at par in four years time. The duration (D) of the bond is calculated as follows:

The redemption yield for this bond is 9% and so the discounting factor $v = 1/1.09 = 0.91743$.

From equation (4.4):

$$D = \frac{1}{100} \times \left(9 \times v + 9 \times 2v^2 + 9 \times 3v^3 + 9 \times 4v^4 + 100 \times 4v^4 \right)$$

$$= 3.531 \text{ years}$$

or from equation (4.5):

$$D = 1 + \frac{9v}{100} \times \left(v + 2v^2 + 3v^3 \right) + \frac{100}{100} \times 3v^4$$

$$= 3.531 \text{ years}$$

It can be seen that for non zero coupon bonds duration does not decrease smoothly for a fixed discount rate when it approaches redemption, as it jumps at every coupon payment.

The graph below shows how the duration of a bond which pays a 10% annual coupon changes over its 6-year life, assuming the price remains at par.

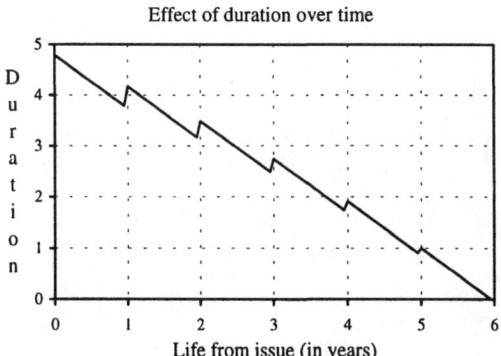

Another feature of duration is that if you increase the maturity date of a bond, assuming that it has the same coupon and redemption yield, then it is possible in certain circumstances for the duration to decrease as opposed to progressively increase. This can occur for long dated bonds with coupons below the assumed redemption yield. It does not occur if the bond is trading above par.

Example ▸

Consider a bond which pays a 5% annual coupon and has a 10% redemption yield. For various lives to maturity it has the durations shown below:

Life to Maturity	Duration
10 years	7.661
20 years	10.741
30 years	11.433
40 years	11.389
50 years	11.236
100 years	11.006

For an undated security, equation (4.5) can be further reduced to:

$$D = \frac{f1}{h} + \frac{g}{P \cdot h^2} \cdot \frac{v^{f1+1}}{(1-v)^2}$$

BOND MARKETS: STRUCTURES AND YIELD CALCULATIONS

$$D = \frac{f1}{h} + \frac{v}{h \cdot (1-v)}$$

$$D = \frac{f1}{h} + \frac{1}{y} \qquad (4.6)$$

This formula for the duration is independent of the coupon.

Example ▸

An undated 8% bond pays interest semi-annually on 15 January and 15 July. On 15 April it has a redemption yield of 10.25% compounded annually. What is its duration?

A yield of 10.25% compounded annually is equivalent to a yield of 10.0% compounded semi-annually (see Appendix II). On 15 April, f1 = 0.5 and the duration (D) is given by:

$$D = \frac{0.5}{2} + \frac{1}{0.1}$$
$$= 10.25 \text{ years}$$

4.7 Modified duration or volatility

The modified duration or volatility of a bond gives the percentage change in price of a bond for a unit change in yield. Hence the larger the modified duration, the greater the price volatility for a specific yield movement.

The modified duration is given by:

$$MD = -\frac{dP}{dy} \cdot \frac{1}{P} \qquad (4.7)$$

where: MD = modified duration
P   = gross price (i.e. clean price plus accrued interest)
dP = small change in price
dy = corresponding small change in yield compounded with the frequency of the coupon payment

It can be easily proved (see Appendix I) that modified duration and duration are related by:

$$MD = D \cdot v \qquad (4.8)$$

where: MD = modified duration
D   = duration

Measures of Life and Associated Calculations

v = discounting factor i.e. if the yield compounded h times per annum is y then $v = 1/(1 + y/h)$ ($y = 0.08$ for a yield of 8%)

h = number of coupon payments per year

Example ▶

A bond paying a 9% annual coupon with four years to go to redemption at par, has been shown to have a duration of 3.531 years if trading at par. The modified duration (MD) is then given by:

$$MD = \frac{3.531}{(1 + 0.09)} = 3.239$$

and so applying equation (4.7) if the yield drops by 0.1% to 8.9% the price should increase by 0.324 to 100.324%.

4.8 Convexity

Modified duration of a bond indicates how the price will change for a small change in yield. Unfortunately, although this works very well for small yield changes it does not for larger changes. This is because the relationship between the price and the yield is not linear, but curvilinear. The degree of curvature, which varies from bond to bond is called the convexity.

Example ▶

Consider a 10 year bond with a 10% annual coupon. Below is a table of prices, actual redemption yields, modified durations and expected yields. The expected yields are calculated using equation (4.7) and are based on the redemption yield and the modified duration when priced at par.

Price	Redemption yield	Modified duration	Expected yield	Difference between yields
90	11.752	5.885	11.627	0.125
95	10.843	6.019	10.814	0.029
99	10.164	6.120	10.163	0.001
99.9	10.016	6.142	10.016	0.000
100	10.000	6.145		
100.1	9.984	6.147	9.984	0.000
101	9.838	6.169	9.837	0.001
105	9.214	6.264	9.186	0.028
110	8.477	6.376	8.373	0.104

Bond Markets: Structures and Yield Calculations

It can be seen that the actual redemption yield for all prices is greater than or equal to the expected yield based on the modified duration.

Mathematically convexity is given by:

$$CX = \frac{1}{P} \cdot \frac{d^2P}{dy^2} \qquad (4.9)$$

where: CX = convexity
P = gross price
y = yield ($y = 0.08$ for a yield of 8%)
and the second derivative of P with respect to y is derived from equation (5.3) which is discussed in the next chapter.

This formula is expanded in Appendix I.

In practice instead of solving equation (4.9) it is usually sufficient to solve the approximation below:

$$CX = 10^6 \cdot (P_1 + P_2 - 2P)/P \qquad (4.10)$$

where: CX = convexity
P = gross price at the current yield
P_1 = gross price of the security if the yield were to increase by 10 basis points (0.1%)
P_2 = gross price of the security if the yield were to decrease by 10 basis points

Example ▶

Using the above example of a 10 year bond priced at par with a 10% annual coupon we have:

P_1 = 99.388174   (yield of 10.1%)
P_2 = 100.617105   (yield of 9.9%)

therefore CX = $10^6 \times (99.388174 + 100.617105 - 200)/100$
= 0.005279×10^4
= 53

CHAPTER 5

YIELDS

Bonds display a variety of anticipated cash flow patterns. For straights and convertibles the cash flow pattern is frequently predictable, with a fixed coupon at regular intervals and redemption on a specific date or dates. However, this is not true for floating rate notes (FRNs) where future cash flows are re-fixed on specified dates relative to a market rate or index (e.g. the London Interbank Offered Rate (LIBOR) for three month U.S. dollars), which varies over time. The methods of evaluating FRNs are discussed in chapter 6.

The wide variation of cash flow patterns for bonds means that prices cannot be used for comparing their relative attractiveness. One of the most common calculations for comparing bonds is that of yield. Three types of yield are commonly used:

- Current yield
- Simple yield to maturity
- Redemption yield

5.1 Current yield

The current yield of a bond is also known as a flat, running or interest yield. It measures the income an investor would receive on a bond, if it continues to pay interest at the current rate, as a percentage of the price of the bond. It does not allow for any appreciation or depreciation that an investor would receive on disposal.

The current yield of a bond is given by the formula:

$$CY = \frac{g \cdot 100}{CP} \qquad (5.1)$$

where: CY = current yield %
  g = annual coupon rate %
  CP = clean price (i.e. not including any accrued interest)

Bond Markets: Structures and Yield Calculations

Example ▸

A bond has a clean price of 98% and a coupon of 9%, then the current yield is:

$$CY = \frac{9 \times 100}{98} = 9.184\%$$

The current yield calculation can be applied to straights, convertibles and FRNs. In the latter case, this is usually based on the last coupon fixing.

5.2 Simple yield to maturity

The simple yield to maturity is also known as a Japanese yield. It takes into account the effect of the capital gain or loss on maturity of the bond as well as the current yield. Unlike the redemption yield calculations any capital appreciation/depreciation is deemed to occur uniformly over the bond's life.

The simple yield to maturity of a bond is given by:

$$SY = \frac{g + (C - CP)/L}{CP} \qquad (5.2)$$

where:
SY = simple yield to maturity (SY = 0.08 for a yield of 8%)
g = annual coupon rate %
CP = clean price
C = redemption value
L = life to maturity in years. This is calculated by taking the number of days to maturity, excluding any 29 February and dividing by 365.

Example ▸

Consider a 6% bond with 3 years 151 days (not counting any potential 29 February) to go to maturity at 100%, which has a clean price of 96%, then the simple yield to maturity is given by:

$$SY = \frac{6 + (100 - 96)/(3 + 151/365)}{96}$$

$$= 0.7471$$

$$= 7.471\%$$

The simple yield to maturity formula (5.2), gives a different value to the simple interest or money market yield formula for a bond, even in the last coupon period *(see section 5.3.2)*.

5.3 Redemption yields

The redemption yield calculation removes the limitations of the current and simple yield to maturity calculations. It allows for all the expected future cash flows from the bond. The cash flows are usually from coupon payments and repayments of capital.

The redemption yield of a bond is that discount rate that would make the sum of the present values of all assumed future cash flows equal to the gross price of the bond. The gross price is the quoted clean price plus any associated accrued interest.

In other words the redemption yield y is given by solving an equation of the form below:

$$P = \sum_{i=1}^{n} CF_i \cdot v^{L_i} \qquad (5.3)$$

where:
- P = gross price (i.e. clean price plus accrued interest)
- n = number of future cash flows
- CF_i = ith cash flow
- L_i = time in periods to the ith cash flow, taking into account the market conventions for calculating the fraction of a period, (e.g. does the year have 360 or 365 days).
- v = discounting factor i.e. $v = 1/(1 + y/h)$
- h = number of periods in the year
- y = required redemption yield compounded h times per annum ($y = 0.08$ for a yield of 8%).

N.B. in the case of partly-paid issues, future price calls are regarded as negative cash flows.

The period refers to the normal compounding period of the market. In the International bond and most European domestic markets this is one year, whereas in the U.K. and U.S. it is 6 months.

This general redemption yield formula, which assumes that all cash flows irrespective of their timing are discounted at the same rate, works for all securities. In addition the ISMA recommend some general principles in its application. These principles can be applied to International and other Domestic bonds.

ISMA Redemption Yield Principles

i) *Unless otherwise specified redemption yields are quoted with an annual compounding period, irrespective of how many coupon periods per annum the bond may have.*

ii) Compound interest is always used for the entire life, even when there is less than one period to redemption.

iii) If the bond accrues interest on a 360-day year then the calendar for all yield calculations consists of a 360-day year.*

iv) Unless otherwise specified, yields are calculated from the assumed value date, not the settlement date (if different) or trade date.

* This rule may be relaxed when applying the ISMA yield calculations to non ISMA securities e.g. one might want to compare the yield on a French Government ECU OAT, which accrues interest on a 365-day year basis, with the yield on a Euro ECU issue. In both cases a 360-day year calendar will normally be assumed for the yield calculations.

Principle (i) above is compatible with the ISMA Rule 803 on a coupon date which states:

Rule 803 Standard maturity yield definition

803.1 The Association's standard method of calculating maturity yields shall be based on the definition of annual interest compounding. i.e. a bond with a 7% coupon, payable annually, priced at 100%, yields 7% per annum and the same bond paying interest semi-annually yields more.

803.2 A member of the Association calculating maturity yields by a method other than the one described above shall state exactly what method has been used for the calculation.

How to solve the general redemption yield formula (5.3) together with the derivation of modified duration and convexity is described in Appendix I.

The general redemption yield formula can be converted into a more manageable form when being applied to specific bonds. For many bonds different redemption yields can be calculated for the same bond with the same price on the same date, according to different assumptions about future cash flows, e.g. whether the bond will be called or not.

Example ▸

Consider the following bond issued by the XYZ Manufacturing Company:

- *it pays an 8% coupon once a year on 1 December;*
- *any outstanding amount will be redeemed at par in four equal amounts on the 1 December 2003, 2004, 2005 and 2006 unless redeemed earlier. Individual bonds are drawn by lot;*

YIELDS

- *it may be called between 1 December 2000 and 1 December 2002 at 102% on 30 days notice;*
- *there is a 'put' option at 100% on 1 December 2001.*

At any date prior to November 2000, the following types of redemption yield calculations could be considered.

i) *Yield to maturity*
   This invariably means final redemption, which in this case is 1 December 2006.

ii) *Yield to average life*
   The weighted average of the normal redemption dates (i.e. 1 June 2005). See discussion on average/equivalent life (section 5.3.5)

iii) *Yield to equivalent life*
    (see section 5.3.5)

iv) *Yield to next call*
    i.e. 1 December 2000 at 102%

v) *Yield to last call*

vi) *Yield to put*

The above options give rise to the concept of an 'Expected Yield', where it is assumed that the issuer will attempt to minimize his costs and the investor will attempt to maximize his return.

Example ▸

In the U.K. Gilt-edged market some of the issues (e.g. Treasury 8% 2002/2006) may be redeemed at any time between two dates at the government's option. It is conventional to quote yields to the earliest date if the clean price of the stock is above par and to the last date if it is below par.

In the above XYZ Manufacturing Company example, the issuer will frequently call the bond if he can raise money at a lower cost after allowing for his expenses and the early call premium. Conversely the holder will exercise his put option on 1 December 2001, if the market price is below par and he can re-invest his capital at a higher return.

5.3.1 Fully paid fixed coupon bond with an assumed single redemption date

For a fully paid fixed coupon bond paying h times per year with an assumed single redemption date, the redemption yield formula (5.3) may be rewritten as:

BOND MARKETS: STRUCTURES AND YIELD CALCULATIONS

$$P = v^{f1} \cdot \left(k + \sum_{i=1}^{n-1} \frac{g}{h} \cdot v^i \right) + \left(C + \frac{g}{h} \cdot f2 \right) \cdot v^{n+f1+f2-1} \qquad (5.4)$$

where:
- P = gross price (i.e. clean price plus accrued interest)
- g = annual coupon rate %
- k = first/next coupon payment %
- h = number of periods in the year.
  So each normal coupon payment is g/h
- n = number of coupon payments to assumed redemption, excluding any fractional payment on redemption
- $f1$ = fraction of a period from value date to the first/next interest payment. A period is defined as the normal time between two consecutive coupon payments
- $f2$ = fraction of a period from the last normal coupon date to the assumed redemption
- C = redemption value
- v = discounting factor i.e. $v = 1/(1 + y/h)$
- y = required redemption yield compounded h times per annum ($y = 0.08$ for a yield of 8%)

It should be noted that solving this equation produces an annualized redemption yield for bonds with annual coupon payments, a semi-annualized yield for bonds with semi-annual coupon payments etc. It is very easy to convert a yield from one compounding frequency to another (see Appendix II).

The above formula calculates the same redemption yield for a semi-annual bond as for an annual bond with half the annual coupon rate, and twice the life. However the yield for the former is per six months and for the latter per year.

This formula can be re-written as:

$$P = v^{f1} \cdot \left\{ k + \frac{g}{h} \cdot \frac{v(1 - v^{n-1})}{(1 - v)} + \left(C + \frac{g}{h} \cdot f2 \right) \cdot v^{n+f2-1} \right\} \qquad (5.5)$$

It can be restated as:

$$P = v^{f1} \cdot \left\{ (C + G \cdot f2) \cdot v^{n+f2-1} + k + \frac{G}{Y} \cdot (1 - v^{n-1}) \right\}$$

where: $Y = y/h$ and $G = g/h$

If we define:
- q = 'adjusted price'
- = $P/v^{f1} - k$
- R = 'adjusted redemption value'
- = $(C + G \cdot f2) \cdot v^{f2}$

and n does not equal 1 this formula can be transformed into:

YIELDS

$$Y = \frac{G}{q} + \frac{(R-q)}{q \cdot x} \quad (5.6)$$

where:
$$x = \frac{\left(1 - v^{n-1}\right)}{Y \cdot v^{n-1}}$$

This formula states that the redemption yield is equal to the current yield plus an income stream which, if re-invested at the yield rate, would at maturity amount to the proportionate capital gain or loss. Since the second factor is relatively insensitive to changes in y when n is greater than 2, the equation is in a form which is suitable for rapid solution by iteration. However, when $n = 2$, the equation sometimes converges very slowly or even diverges. In these circumstances a more appropriate re-arrangement of equation (5.5) which converges quickly is:

$$Y = \left\{\frac{(G+R) \cdot v}{P} + \frac{k}{P}\right\}^{1/f1} - 1 \quad (5.7)$$

If $n = 1$ the yield equation (5.5) can be re-written:

$$Y = \left\{\frac{R+k}{P}\right\}^{1/f1} - 1 \quad (5.8)$$

Yields on bonds in their last coupon period (i.e. where $n = 1$) are described further in section 5.3.2.

There are many other ways of solving the redemption yield equation. For example, the Newton-Raphson iterative method could be used, (see Appendix I).

The number of iterations required to solve the yield equation (5.6), (5.7) or (5.8) is dependent on the accuracy of the initial approximation which is substituted in the right hand side of the equation.

An initial approximation which gives reasonable results is:

$$Y_o = \frac{G}{CP} + \left\{\frac{C}{CP}\right\}^{1/L} - 1 \quad (5.9)$$

where:
- Y_o = initial approximation
- G = normal coupon payment % for the compounding period
- C = redemption value
- CP = clean price
- L = life = $n + f1 + f2 - 1$

The above formula can be applied to calculate yields to maturity, call, extension and put, and for bonds with sinking funds, yields to average life.

BOND MARKETS: STRUCTURES AND YIELD CALCULATIONS

Example ▶

Consider the above XYZ Manufacturing Company 8% bond where:

- *the interest is paid annually on 1 December;*
- *the issue will be redeemed at par in four equal instalments on 1 December 2003, 2004, 2005 & 2006;*
- *the first call opportunity is on 1 December 2000 at 102%;*
- *the bond holder has a put option at 100% on 1 December 2001.*

If, for value date 1 September 1997, it has a price of 92%, the following redemption yields could be calculated:

To maturity	(1 December 2006)	9.317%
To average life	(1 June 2005)	9.500%
To next call	(1 December 2000 at 102%)	11.603%
To put	(1 December 2001)	10.401%

The redemption yield formula (5.4) above, implies that the yield of a bond varies throughout its life between coupon payments, even if the clean price is always par. This is illustrated in the following graph, which shows the yields for a bond with a 7% annual coupon, with a price throughout its 4-year life of par.

Change in redemption yield over time

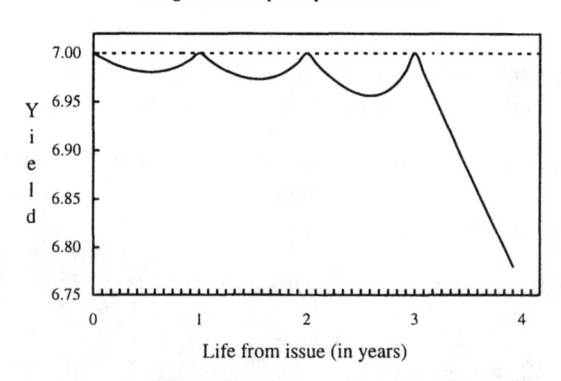

Yield vs. Life from issue (in years)

5.3.2 Money Market yields (Bonds in their last coupon period)

In some markets bond yields are calculated in the last coupon period on a simple interest, rather than on a compound interest basis.

The normal compound redemption yield formula (5.4) reduces in the last coupon period to:

$$P = \left\{\frac{g}{h} + C\right\} \cdot v^{f1} \qquad (5.10)$$

where:
- P = gross price (i.e. clean price plus accrued interest)
- g = annual coupon rate
- h = number of coupon payments per year. In this case it has been assumed that a normal coupon g/h is paid at redemption.
- $f1$ = fraction of a period from value date to the redemption date. A period is defined as the normal time between two consecutive coupon payments
- C = redemption value
- v = discounting factor i.e. $v = 1/(1 + y/h)$
- y = required redemption yield compounded h times per annum ($y = 0.08$ for a yield of 8%)

The formula (5.10) may be re-written as:

$$P \cdot \left\{1 + \frac{y}{h}\right\}^{f1} = \frac{g}{h} + C \qquad (5.11)$$

This formula can be expanded to:

$$P \cdot \left\{1 + \frac{f1 \cdot y}{h} + \frac{f1 \cdot (f1-1) \cdot y^2}{2h^2} + \cdots\right\} = \frac{g}{h} + C$$

For markets which use simple interest in the last period, formula (5.11) is replaced by:

$$P \cdot \left\{1 + \frac{f1 \cdot MMY}{h}\right\} = \frac{g}{h} + C$$

In this revised formula *MMY* is known as the 'money market yield'.

This formula may be re-stated as:

$$P = \frac{\frac{g}{h} + C}{1 + MMY \cdot \frac{d}{a}}$$

$$MMY = \frac{\left(\frac{g}{h} + C - P\right)}{P} \cdot \frac{a}{d} \qquad (5.12)$$

BOND MARKETS: STRUCTURES AND YIELD CALCULATIONS

where: d = number of days according to the relevant calendar until redemption

a = number of days in an relevant calendar year. (This could be 360, 365 or 365/366, however there are other variants)

as $f1/h$ = d/a

From the formulae above, it can be seen that it is easy to convert from a redemption yield (using compounding) to a money market yield and vice versa.

The relationship is:

$$(1 + y/h)^{f1} = (1 + MMY \cdot f1/h)$$

If $f1 = 1$ then $y = MMY$, so there is no discontinuity in moving from a compound redemption yield to a simple interest money market yield at the beginning of the last period.

Example ▸

If a security with 6 months to redemption has an annually compounded redemption yield (y) of 8%, then it will have a money market yield (MMY) given by:

$$(1 + 0.08/1)^{0.5} = (1 + MMY \times 0.5)$$

$$MMY = \left(1.08^{0.5} - 1\right) \times 2$$
$$= 0.07846$$
$$= 7.846\%$$

This is exactly the same relationship as that between a semi-annually compounded yield of 7.846% and an annually compounded yield of 8%, (see Appendix II).

Money market calculations are discussed further in chapter 9. The money market yield calculation is different to the simple yield to maturity given in equation (5.2), which uses a clean as opposed to a gross price.

Example ▸

Consider a bond which pays an annual coupon of 8% on 30 September each year, and is redeemed at par on 30 September 1998. The bond is quoted with a clean price of 99%.

YIELDS

A comparison of compound interest and money market simple interest yields, based on a 360 day year, is given below for various dates.

Value Date	Life (Years)	Gross Price %	Bond Yield	Money Market Yield
30 September 1997	1.00	99	9.091%	9.091%
30 December 1997	0.75	101	9.346%	9.241%
30 March 1998	0.50	103	9.944%	9.709%
30 June 1998	0.25	105	11.928%	11.429%

N.B. the money market yield, based on a 360-day year calendar, is equivalent to an ISMA bond yield that has been compounded with the frequency of its life. Thus, in the above table, for a life to maturity of six months, the annualized bond yield of 9.944% is equivalent to a semi-annual yield of 9.709% (see section 5.3.7), which is the money market yield equivalent.

5.3.3 Zero coupon bonds

For zero coupon bonds the redemption yield formula (5.3) reduces to:

$$P = C \cdot v^{n+f1-1} \tag{5.13}$$

if one treats it, for the purpose of calculating $f1$ and n, as a bond which pays zero coupons once a year on an anniversary of the redemption date. This automatically implies that $f2 = 0$ and the clean price CP is the same as the gross price P.

$n + f1 - 1$ is just the life L of the bond in years, hence equation (5.13) may be rewritten as:

$$y = \left\{\frac{C}{CP}\right\}^{1/L} - 1$$

which is the same as the initial approximation (5.9) for fixed coupon bonds. Hence iterations are not necessary to establish the redemption yields of zero coupon bonds.

Example ▶

The XYZ Manufacturing Company has issued a zero coupon bond which will be redeemed at par on 1 November 2008. On the 28 April 1998 it is trading in the secondary market at a price of 30%, with a value date of 1 May 1998.

The life (L) of the bond from the value date to redemption is 10.5 years hence the redemption yield (y) is given by:

$$y = (100/30)^{1/10.5} - 1 = 0.12150 = 12.150\%$$

BOND MARKETS: STRUCTURES AND YIELD CALCULATIONS

5.3.4 Undated securities

The formula for undated securities (perpetuals) assumes that the capital will never be repaid and the issuer will never default on coupon payments.

Based on these assumptions the redemption yield formula (5.3) reduces to:

$$P = v^{f1} \cdot \left\{ k + \frac{g}{h} \cdot \left(v + v^2 + v^3 + \cdots \right) \right\}$$

$$P = v^{f1} \cdot \left\{ k + \frac{g \cdot v}{h \cdot (1 - v)} \right\}$$

$$P = v^{f1} \cdot \left\{ k + \frac{g}{y} \right\} \tag{5.14}$$

where:
- P = gross price (i.e. clean price plus accrued interest)
- g = annual coupon rate %
- k = first/next coupon payment %
- h = number of periods in the year. So each normal coupon payment is g/h
- $f1$ = fraction of a period from value date to the first/next interest payment. A period is defined as the normal time between two consecutive coupon payments
- v = discounting factor i.e. $v = 1/(1 + y/h)$
- y = required redemption yield compounded h times per annum ($y = 0.08$ for a yield of 8%)

The equation (5.14) can be solved as described in the Appendix I or as:

$$y = \frac{g}{\left(\dfrac{P}{v^{f1}} - k \right)} \tag{5.15}$$

which can be solved by iteration with an initial approximation y_0 in the right hand side of:

$$y_0 = \frac{g}{CP}$$

It should be noted that equation (5.14) on a normal coupon date, when there is no accrued interest and $f1 = 1$, reduces to:

$$y = \frac{g}{P} = \frac{g}{CP}$$

Example ▶

Consider an undated bond which pays an annual coupon of 7% on 1 December each year. If on 25 May the bond is trading at a price of 90% for a value date of 1 June 1998 then, assuming a standard coupon payment of 7% on 1 December 1998, the redemption yield (y) is given by solving:

$$y = \frac{7}{(90 + 7 \times 0.5)/v^{0.5} - 7}$$

where: $v = 1/(1 + y)$

This gives: $y = 7.772\%$

5.3.5 Bonds with sinking funds (yields to average/equivalent life)

For bonds with sinking funds, the ISMA convention used to be to calculate redemption yields to the average life of the bond. In doing so, the formula assumes that the bond is completely redeemed on one date, which is the average date of the non-discounted capital repayments and that the bond pays a full coupon up to that date. This distorts the actual cash flows of the bond, and hence does not calculate a true redemption yield. However, it does mean that the single date redemption yield formula can be applied.

Example ▶

Consider an 8% bond which pays annual coupons on 1 December each year and is redeemed at par in four equal instalments on 1 December 1999 to 2002. The assumed average life and the true cash flows from 1 December 1994 are as follows:

Date	'Average Life' Payments			Actual Payments		
	Coupon %	Capital %	Total %	Coupon %	Capital %	Total %
1 December 1994	8	-	8	8	-	8
Repeated each year until						
1 December 1998	8	-	8	8	-	8
1 December 1999	8	-	8	8	25	33
1 December 2000	8	-	8	6	25	31
1 June 2001	4	100	104	-	-	-
1 December 2001	-	-	-	4	25	29
1 December 2002	-	-	-	2	25	27

BOND MARKETS: STRUCTURES AND YIELD CALCULATIONS

In the above table, the average redemption date is 1 June 2001 as the bond is redeemed in four equal instalments. On this date there is assumed to be a fractional coupon payment of 4%, being six months accrued interest.

N.B. the actual coupon payments decrease after part of the bond has been redeemed.

It can be seen in the above example and generally that the average life and the actual coupon and capital repayments total to the same amount in both cases, although the timings are obviously different.

It is not the convention to calculate redemption yields for bonds with purchase funds, as opposed to sinking funds in this way, since the existence of the purchase fund does not affect the expected cash flows of a long term holder of the bond.

The redemption yield calculation which discounts all the actual coupon and capital payments in the same way is often referred to as the redemption yield to equivalent life. It should be noted that this yield is not the same as that of a similar bullet bond which is redeemed on the equivalent life date (see section 4.5).

The formula for calculating the redemption yield to equivalent life of a bond with a fixed coupon, where all capital repayments are made on a coupon date, can be written as:

$$P = v^{f1} \cdot \{R_1 + R_2 \cdot v + R_3 \cdot v^2 + \cdots + R_n \cdot v^{n-1}\} \qquad (5.16)$$

where:
- P = gross price (i.e. clean price plus accrued interest)
- g = annual coupon rate %
- k = first/next coupon payment %
- h = number of periods in the year. So each normal coupon payment is g/h
- n = number of coupon payments to final redemption
- $f1$ = fraction of a period from value date to the first/next coupon payment. A period is defined as the normal time between two consecutive coupon payments
- C_i = percentage of the issue redeemed with the ith coupon payment
- R_1 = $k + C_1$
- R_i = $C_i + (1 - F_i) \cdot g/h$ for $i = 2$ to n
- F_i = fraction of the issue redeemed prior to the coupon date. For an issue redeemed at par F_i is given by:

$$F_i = \frac{\sum_{j=1}^{i-1} C_j}{\sum_{j=1}^{n} C_j}$$

YIELDS

v = discounting factor i.e. $v = 1/(1 + y/h)$
y = required redemption yield compounded h times per annum ($y = 0.08$ for a yield of 8%)

In practice, it is probably easier to solve the general redemption yield formula (see Appendix I), than this one.

Example ▸

Consider the following 9% U.S. dollar bond which pays annual coupons on 30 September each year and is redeemed in two equal instalments at par on 30 September 1999 and 30 September 2000.

On the 27 March 1998 it is trading at a price of 98 1/8% for a value date of 30 March 1998.

It can be shown that the yield to equivalent life of the bond is 10.024% since as the accrued interest is 4.5%, equation (5.16) becomes:

$$(98.125 + 4.5) = \frac{1}{1.10024^{0.5}} \times \left(9 + \frac{(50 + 9)}{1.10024} + \frac{(50 + 4.5)}{1.10024^2}\right)$$

On the other hand the yield to average life is 10.070% as the equation to solve is now (5.5) which gives:

$$(98.125 + 4.5) = \frac{1}{1.10070^{0.5}} \times \left(9 + \frac{9}{1.10070} + \frac{(100 + 4.5)}{1.10070^{1.5}}\right)$$

In the above equation the average life redemption date is 30 March 2000.

5.3.6 Other bond types

The general redemption yield formula (5.3) can be used for securities that have features that are not described in the previous sections.

For example it can be used for partly paid securities and graduated rate bonds.

The formula for a partly paid security redeemed on a single redemption date may be written as:

$$P + \sum_{i=1}^{j} R_i \cdot v^{ci} = v^{f1} \cdot \left(k + \sum_{i=1}^{n-1} \frac{g}{h} \cdot v^i\right) + \left(C + \frac{g}{h} \cdot f2\right) \cdot v^{n+f1+f2-1} \quad (5.17)$$

where: P = gross partly paid price (i.e. market price plus accrued interest)
R_i = future calls for $i = 1$ to j

BOND MARKETS: STRUCTURES AND YIELD CALCULATIONS

j = number of future calls
ci = the time in periods from the value date to the ith call
g = annual coupon rate %
k = first/next coupon payment %
h = number of coupon payments per year. So each normal coupon payment is g/h
n = number of coupon payments to final redemption
$f1$ = fraction of a period from value date to the first/next payment. A period is defined as the normal time between two consecutive coupon payments
$f2$ = fraction of a period from the last normal coupon date to the assumed redemption
C = redemption value
v = discounting factor i.e. $v = 1/(1 + y/h)$
y = required redemption yield compounded h times per annum ($y = 0.08$ for a yield of 8%)

Using similar notation the redemption yield formula for a graduated rate bond which pays a coupon rate of g_1 for the first $(m-1)$ payments after the first and a coupon rate of g_2 for the remaining $(n-m)$ payments is:

$$P = v^{f1} \cdot \left\{ k + \sum_{i=1}^{m-1} \frac{g_1}{h} \cdot v^i + \sum_{i=m}^{n-1} \frac{g_2}{h} \cdot v^i \right\} + \left\{ C + \frac{g}{h} \cdot f2 \right\} \cdot v^{n+f1+f2-1} \quad (5.18)$$

It can be seen that both these formulae are very similar to equation 5.4.

Formulae can be created in a similar way for securities with irregular coupon payments, dual currency bonds based on some assumptions of future exchange rates, and even indexed bonds.

5.3.7 Other redemption yields

Some markets use 'redemption yields' that do not agree with the previously discussed formulae.

The most common method uses simple interest for the first broken period and compound interest thereafter.

Variations of this method are those of the U.S. Federal Reserve (not the U.S. 'Street' method) and the German Braess-Fangmeyer and Moosmüller approaches.

The general redemption yield formula (5.3):

$$P = \sum_{i=1}^{n} CF_i \cdot v^{Li}$$

where: P = gross price (i.e. clean price plus accrued interest)
n = number of future cash flows

CF_i	=	ith cash flow
L_i	=	time in periods to the ith cash flow
v	=	discounting factor
		i.e. if the yield is y then $v = 1/(1+y/h)$
		($y = 0.08$ for a yield of 8%)
h	=	number of periods per year

is effectively replaced by:

$$P = \sum_{i=1}^{n} \frac{CF_i \cdot v^{i-1}}{(1 + f1 \cdot y)}$$

if the ith cash flow CF_i has an outstanding life L_i which is equal to $n+f1-1$, where $f1$ is the fraction of a period from the value date to the first/next interest payment.

In other words instead of discounting each cash flow which is $(n-1)$ periods plus a fractional period $f1$ in the future by:

$$(1 + y)^{n+f1-1}$$

it is discounted at the rate:

$$(1 + f1 \cdot y) \cdot (1 + y)^{n-1}$$

CHAPTER 6

FLOATING RATE NOTE CALCULATIONS

In order to apply the standard redemption yield calculations to floating rate notes (FRNs), one has to make assumptions about future coupon payments. This is obviously a very difficult thing to do accurately, with the result that a different approach is frequently used.

Most floating rate notes have a known first/next coupon payment, while subsequent coupons will usually be set in terms of a margin over a specified indicator rate (e.g. the London Interbank Offered Rate (LIBOR) for three month U.S. dollars). As a result a current margin relative to the indicator rate is often calculated.

Two types of margin calculations are described below:

Simple Margins and Discounted Margins. Margin calculations enable FRNs to be compared with each other and with money market instruments, but not with fixed rate bonds. In order to facilitate bond comparisons a yield formula is also given in section 6.3.

6.1 Simple margin

The simple margin formula measures the return that can be obtained on the FRN relative to the indicator rate. Its calculation consists of two parts:

- the quoted margin of the security above or below the indicator rate;

- the average annual capital gain or loss to redemption, after allowing for differences in the indicator between the last coupon fixing date and the trade date.

FLOATING RATE NOTE CALCULATIONS

The simple margin is given by the formula:

$$SM = \frac{C - \text{Adjusted Price}}{L} + QM \quad (6.1)$$

where: SM = simple margin %
         C = redemption value
         L = life of the FRN in years
         QM = quoted margin %

and where the price is adjusted for differences in the current indicator rate and that set at the last coupon fixing.

There are various ways that the price may be adjusted for interest rate changes, however, a method which does not have any discontinuities is shown in the simple margin calculation below:

$$SM = \frac{C - \left(P + (I + QM) \cdot f1 - k\right)}{L} + QM \quad (6.2.)$$

where: SM = simple margin %
         C = redemption value
         P = gross price (i.e. clean price plus accrued interest)
         I = indicator rate to the next coupon date %
         QM = quoted margin %
         $f1$ = fraction of a year from the value date to the first/next coupon date (actual days divided by 360, 365 or 365/366-days according to the issue)
         k = first/next coupon payment %
         L = life in years (actual days/assumed number of days in a year)

In most currencies, including U.S. dollars but not sterling, it is conventional to quote margins on the basis of a 360-day year. Thus in the above formula it is desirable to convert any capital gain or loss onto the same basis. Hence for U.S. dollars the life is based on actual days from value date to redemption divided by 360.

In the Euro-sterling market, the quoted margins usually refer to a rate based on a 365-day year or 366-days in a leap year. A year for the life calculations may be taken to be 365.25 days.

It should be noted that sterling floating rate certificates of deposit accrue interest on the basis of actual days divided by 365 even in a leap year.

BOND MARKETS: STRUCTURES AND YIELD CALCULATIONS

Example ▶

Consider the following U.S. dollar FRN which is redeemed at par on 31 May 2003. It pays interest on 31 May and 30 November each year at 0.25% above the six month LIBOR for U.S. dollars. On the 30 November 1997 the coupon to be paid on 31 May 1998 was set relative to a six month LIBOR rate of 9%. If on the 30 January 1998 the LIBOR rate to 31 May 1998 is 8% and the FRN is being traded at a price of 98%, then the simple margin is calculated as follows:

$$k = (9 + 0.25) \times \frac{182}{360} = 4.67639 \text{ as there are 182 days in the period}$$

$$f1 = \frac{121}{360} = 0.33611 \qquad \text{121 days from settlement to coupon date}$$

$$L = (365 + 365 + 366 + 365 + 365 + 121)/360 = 5.40833$$

$$P = 98 + (9 + 0.25) \times \frac{61}{360} = 99.56736$$

$$SM = \frac{100 - (99.56736 + (8 + 0.25) \times 0.33611 - 4.67639) + 0.25}{5.40833}$$

$$= \frac{100 - 97.66388}{5.40833} + 0.25 = 0.682\%$$

6.2 Discounted margin

The simple margin formula discussed in section 6.1 has two significant drawbacks. It does not allow for the current yield effect on the margin if the price is above or below par, and it assumes that any capital gain or loss occurs evenly over the life of the note, as opposed to being compounded at a constant rate.

The discounted margin formula overcomes these drawbacks, however, in order to make it easier to compute, it is desirable to assume that all coupons after the first one are paid with a constant frequency period.

Floating rate notes (FRNs) in the international and some domestic markets tend to pay interest on different days each year, with the coupon being based on the actual number of days between the coupon dates, which may vary, (see chapters 2 and 11).

The coupons paid after the first/next one, which has already been declared, are all assumed to be the same. Each one being the assumed annual coupon rate, adjusted for the number of days in the year (by convention for FRNs other than Eurosterling this is assumed to be 365.25 days) divided by the number of payments per year.

FLOATING RATE NOTE CALCULATIONS

The discounted margin for FRNs redeemed on a normal coupon date may be obtained by solving:

$$P \cdot \left(1 + \frac{(I + DM)}{100} \cdot f1\right) = k + \sum_{i=1}^{n-1} \frac{(I2 + QM)}{h} \cdot v^i + C \cdot v^{n-1} \qquad (6.3)$$

where:
DM = required discounted margin %
P = gross price (i.e. clean price plus accrued interest)
I = current market indicator rate from the value date to the first coupon date %
$I2$ = assumed market indicator rate for subsequent coupon payments %
$f1$ = fraction of a year from the value date to the first/next coupon date (actual days divided by 360, 365 or 365/366 days according to the issue)

k = first/next coupon payment %
n = number of future coupon payments
QM = quoted margin %
h = number of coupon payments per year adjusted if not Euro-sterling for the assumed number of days in the year e.g. for a U.S. dollar FRN with two coupon payments per year, h will be $2 \times 360/365.25$
C = redemption value
v = discounting factor i.e. $v = 1/(1 + (I2 + DM)/100h)$

In the above formula it can be seen that the left hand side is just the cost of the security adjusted using current indicator rates to the first coupon date.

Similarly each coupon payment after the first is assumed to be $(I2 + QM)/h$.

Equation (6.3) can be compared with equation (5.4) for fixed rate bonds. The major difference being that the period to the first coupon date now uses simple interest as opposed to compound interest throughout, as in equation (5.19).

Example ▶

Consider the same U.S. dollar FRN as that used in the simple margin calculation example. It pays interest on 31 May and 30 November each year at 1/4% above the six month LIBOR for U.S. dollars, and will be redeemed at par on 31 May 2003. The coupon to be paid on 31 May 1998 was set relative to a LIBOR rate of 9%. On 30 January 1998 the LIBOR rate to 31 May 1998 is 8% and the FRN is being traded at a price of 98%. If it is assumed that the LIBOR for six month dollars during the life of the bond is 8% then the discounted margin (DM) is given by solving:

BOND MARKETS: STRUCTURES AND YIELD CALCULATIONS

$$(98 + 1.56736) \times \left(1 + \frac{8 + DM}{100} \cdot \frac{121}{360}\right) = 4.67639$$

$$+ \sum_{i=1}^{10} \frac{(8 + 0.25)}{1.971253} \cdot v^i + 100 \cdot v^{10}$$

where: $\quad v = \dfrac{1}{1 + \left(\dfrac{8 + DM}{197.1253}\right)}$

This gives DM = 0.789%

For undated FRNs (perpetuals) the discounted margin formula (6.3) simplifies to:

$$P \cdot \left(1 + \frac{I + DM}{100} \cdot f1\right) = k + 100 \cdot \left(\frac{I2 + QM}{I2 + DM}\right) \qquad (6.4)$$

Example ▸

Consider an undated U.S. dollar FRN on 31 March, which pays coupons every six months on 31 March and 30 September. It pays interest at 1/4% over six month U.S. dollar LIBOR, and is currently trading at 99%. The current LIBOR rate is 9 3/4% p.a. and the first interest payment is:

$$(9.75 + 0.25) \times 183 / 360 = 5.083\%$$

If both I and I2 are taken to be 9.75%, the discounted margin (DM) is given by:

$$99 \times \left(1 + \frac{(9.75 + DM)}{100} \times \frac{183}{360}\right) = 5.083 + 100 \times \frac{(9.75 + 0.25)}{(9.75 + DM)}$$

which gives:

$$DM = 0.351\%$$

6.3 Yields

The calculation of current and redemption yields enable floating rate notes (FRNs) to be compared with fixed rate bonds.

The calculation of a current yield is the same as for a fixed rate bond, although any calculations are only valid up to the next coupon payment.

On the other hand the general redemption yield formula (5.3) can be applied to FRNs as below.

It can be re-written:

$$P = \sum_{i=1}^{n} k_i \cdot v^{f1+ti} + C \cdot v^{f1+tn} \qquad (6.5)$$

where:
- P = gross price (i.e. clean price plus accrued interest)
- h = number of coupon payments per year
- n = number of coupon payments to assumed redemption
- $f1$ = fraction of a period from value date to the first/next coupon payment. A period is defined as the normal time between two consecutive coupon payments
- C = redemption value
- k_i = assumed ith coupon payment %
- t_i = time in periods from the next to the ith coupon payment
- v = discounting factor i.e. $v = 1/(1 + y/h)$
- y = required redemption yield compounded h times per annum ($y = 0.08$ for a yield of 8%)

To solve this equation satisfactorily means that future coupon rates have to be predicted. One objective way is to assume that the current rates will not change in the future.

This formula can be simplified if it is assumed that all future coupon dates are equidistant and redemption occurs on a normal coupon date. Equation (6.5) can then be re-written:

$$P = v^{f1} \cdot \left\{ k + \sum_{i=1}^{n-1} \frac{g}{h} \cdot v^i + C \cdot v^{n-1} \right\} \qquad (6.6)$$

where:
- k = known first/next coupon payment %
- g = assumed adjusted annual coupon rate, for payments after the known first coupon payment.
  Rates, which are quoted on the basis of a 360-day year, are multiplied by 365.25/360

Equation (6.6) now looks very similar to equation (5.4) for fixed rate bonds and can be solved in a similar way.

Example ▶

Consider a U.S. dollar FRN, which pays interest on 15 March, June, September and December each year until redemption on 15 December 2007 at par. It pays interest at

BOND MARKETS: STRUCTURES AND YIELD CALCULATIONS

a 1/4% over three month LIBOR for U.S. dollars. The current LIBOR rate is 8%, and the next interest payment on 15 March 1998 was set at 2%, based on a LIBOR rate of 7 3/4%. It is trading for a value date of 15 January 1998 at 98%.

There are 90 days between 15 December 1997 and 15 March 1998, so the accrued interest on 15 January 1998 is:

$$2 \times 31/90 = 0.689\%$$

Hence:
$P = 98 + 0.689$
$k = 2$
$g = (8 + 0.25) \times 365.25/360 = 8.3703$
$n = 40$

This gives a redemption yield compounded quarterly of 8.663%, or compounded annually of 8.949%, (see Appendix II).

CHAPTER 7

CONVERTIBLE CALCULATIONS

Convertible bonds are securities that give the holder the option to convert into another security at predefined dates and rates. The rates are normally subject to adjustment in the event of certain capital changes which affect the underlying security. The new security is usually an equity share.

In addition to the normal bond calculations, it is possible to calculate conversion ratios, exercise costs, conversion premiums or discounts, income differentials, break-even periods and value the option itself. There are many methods of valuing options, which are not discussed in this book.

7.1. Conversion premium/discount - ratio

The conversion terms of an issue usually give the holder the right to convert stock into shares between specific dates. With the exception of Swiss convertibles (discussed below) there is normally no cash adjustment at the time of conversion. Fractions on conversion are usually ignored.

When the conversion is exercised any accrued interest on the bond is lost, although the holder is frequently entitled to the next equity dividend payment.

The conversion price is the nominal value of the convertible which may be exchanged for one share. The conversion price is normally quoted in the currency of the equity share. If the convertible bond is in a different currency to the share, a fixed exchange rate for converting from one currency to the other will usually have been agreed at the time of issue.

The conversion ratio is simply the number of shares into which each bond may be converted i.e. assuming they are in the same currency it is the bond denomination divided by the conversion price.

BOND MARKETS: STRUCTURES AND YIELD CALCULATIONS

The exercise cost of purchasing an equity share via a convertible in the currency of the equity is given by:

$$EC = \frac{P \cdot PC \cdot CR}{100 \cdot FR} \qquad (7.1)$$

where: EC = exercise cost
P = gross price of the bond (i.e clean price plus accrued interest)
PC = conversion price (in the currency of the share)
FR = fixed exchange rate, expressed in units of the underlying equity currency that can be purchased for one unit of the bond denominated currency e.g. if a U.S. dollar convertible bond is convertible into Japanese yen shares at the rate of USD 1 = JPY 125 then the rate will be 125
CR = current exchange rate, expressed as above

If the convertible and the shares are in the same currency FR and CR are both 1.

This exercise cost (EC) can be compared with the cost of buying the equity share directly, to give a premium/discount.

The conversion premium/discount % is given by:

$$PM = \left\{ \frac{P \cdot PC \cdot CR}{100 \cdot SP \cdot FR} - 1 \right\} \cdot 100 \qquad (7.2)$$

where: PM = conversion premium/discount %
SP = share price

In the above the conversion premium/discount calculation uses the gross price as any accrued interest on the bond is lost on conversion, however the market often quotes the premium/discount on clean bond prices.

Example ▸

Consider the following bond:

Kinki Sogo Bank 2.875% USD convertible bonds due 31 March 2003 with semi-annual payments

Bond price	-	USD	124.0%
Accrued interest for settlement on 8 March 1989			
(158 days accrued interest)	-	USD	1.262%
Conversion price	-	JPY	1069.1
Share price	-	JPY	1500.0
Current exchange rate	-	JPY	146.75 = USD 1
Fixed exchange rate	-	JPY	130.20 = USD 1

Conversion premium/discount including accrued interest in the convertible bond price.

$$= \left\{ \frac{125.262 \times 1069.1 \times 146.75}{100 \times 1500 \times 130.2} - 1 \right\} \times 100$$

$$= 0.627\%$$

Conversion premium/discount excluding accrued interest in the convertible bond price.

$$= \left\{ \frac{124 \times 1069.1 \times 146.75}{100 \times 1500 \times 130.2} - 1 \right\} \times 100$$

$$= -0.387\%$$

It is normal for conversion terms to be protected and adjusted if there is a capital change such as a scrip or rights issue in the underlying equity shares.

Swiss convertibles differ from most other convertible issues in that when the bonds are converted there is frequently a cash adjustment, which represents the dilution or increase in the conversion price following a capital change.

Example ▶

Paribas Suisse (Bahamas) Ltd. 6 1/4% 1990 debentures of USD 1225 convert into five bearer shares of Banque Paribas (Suisse) S.A. of CHF 100 each and USD 562.34 of cash.

In order to calculate the premium/discount on such a Swiss convertible the convertible price must first be reduced by the cash payment. Similar partly convertible bonds are not unknown in the domestic bond markets.

7.2 Income differential and break-even period

The optimal date to convert a bond into the underlying equity share, subject to the timing of individual coupon and dividend payments, is usually as soon as the income from holding the equity shares is expected to be greater than that of holding the convertible bonds. There may of course be reasons why a holder might not wish to convert under such circumstances e.g. tax considerations or the equity dividend is not expected to be maintained.

If one assumes no change in equity dividends, then the optimal conversion date for a security that does not vary its conversion terms over time, is either the first or last opportunity. In practice this is not the case and people frequently assume annual

BOND MARKETS: STRUCTURES AND YIELD CALCULATIONS

percentage rises in equity dividends, which give rise to optimal conversion dates in the middle of the conversion period.

A break-even period can be calculated, which measures the number of years one would have to hold the convertible before the additional income received on the convertible compared with the equity, assuming no change in dividend, compensates for the conversion premium paid. It does not allow for the differences in the timings of the cash flows.

The break-even period for a convertible and equity in the same currency is given by the formula:

$$BE = \frac{EC - SP}{\left(g \cdot \frac{PC}{100} - d\right)} \quad (7.3)$$

where:
- BE = break-even period in years
- EC = exercise cost of purchasing one share via the convertible
- SP = share price
- PC = conversion price
- g = annual convertible coupon rate %
- d = gross equity dividend payment

The numerator in equation (7.3) is just the additional cost of purchasing a share via the convertible as opposed to directly, whilst the denominator is the loss of income (income differential) per share.

Example ▸

An XYZ Company 8% sterling issue is convertible into XYZ ordinary shares at a conversion price of GBP 4.00 per share. The ordinary shares currently pay a gross dividend of 20p per annum, and are trading in the market at GBP 3.80. The current price of the convertible is 105%.

The exercise cost (EC) of a share is: $105 \times 4 / 100 = 4.20$

The income differential per share is: $8 \times 4 / 100 - 0.20 = 0.12$

Hence the break-even period is: $\frac{4.20 - 3.80}{0.12} = 3.33$ years

---

In the above example, if one were to forecast that the equity dividend would increase by 2p per year after the current year then the 'break even' period, ignoring any cash flow timings would increase to 5 years. This is because the income differentials in each of the first 5 years would be 12p, 10p, 8p, 6p and 4p respectively, which add up to 40p which is the difference between the exercise cost and the share price.

CHAPTER 8

WARRANTS

A warrant gives the holder the right to purchase an asset at a defined price between specified dates. The same terms usually apply to the entire exercise period, although there is normally protection against changes in the underlying asset. The asset on which there is an option could be a bond, an equity share, an index, a commodity, a currency, or any other financial instrument.

8.1 Bond warrants

A bond warrant gives the holder the right to purchase bonds with a face value of EV (exercise value) at a percentage price of EP (exercise price). The bonds issued on exercise of the warrants could be either a further tranche of an existing issue or a new issue.

In other words the exercise cost of purchasing the underlying bond via the warrant is given by:

$$EC = \left\{ WP \cdot CR + \frac{EP \cdot EV}{100} \right\} \cdot \frac{100}{EV} \qquad (8.1)$$

where:
- EC = exercise cost in the currency of the underlying bond
- WP = warrant price
- CR = current exchange rate, expressed in units of the bond currency that can be purchased for one unit of the warrant currency. If they are the same currency then $CR = 1$
- EP = exercise price of the bond (% price basis)
- EV = face (par) value of the underlying bonds which may be purchased per warrant

In the international bond market, it is normal to express bond warrant prices as the actual cost of the warrant.

BOND MARKETS: STRUCTURES AND YIELD CALCULATIONS

When the warrant is exercised the purchaser has to pay in addition to the exercise price the accrued interest at that date.

Example ▸

London and Scottish Marine Oil PLC - warrant to subscribe for USD 9 1/2% bonds due 1996.

Each warrant will entitle the holder to subscribe for USD 1,000 principal amount of the Company's 9 1/2% bond due 1996 at the exercise price of 100 percent of the principal amount plus accrued interest from the preceding 12 July. The warrants will be exercisable up to and including 12 July 1992.

If the warrants are priced at USD 24, the exercise cost (EC) of purchasing the USD 1000 principal amount of the 9 1/2% bonds will be:

$$EC = (24 + (100 \times 1000)/100) \times 100/1000$$

$$= 102.4\% \text{ plus any accrued interest}$$

If the warrant gives the holder the right to purchase a bond which already exists a premium/discount of purchasing the bond via the warrant as opposed to directly may be calculated.

The premium/discount is given by:

$$PM = \left\{\frac{EC}{CP} - 1\right\} \cdot 100 \qquad (8.2)$$

where: PM = warrant premium/discount %
         EC = exercise cost
         CP = clean price of the underlying bond

N.B. in this formula the clean price is used as the purchaser has to pay any accrued interest when the warrant is exercised.

Example ▸

If in the above London and Scottish Marine Oil example, the 9 1/2% bonds exist and are trading at 98%, as the exercise cost of the bonds via the warrant is 102.4%, the premium (PM) is:

$$PM = \left\{\frac{102.4}{98} - 1\right\}$$

$$= 4.490\%$$

8.2 Equity warrants

If an equity warrant gives the holder the right to purchase n shares at a price of EP per share, then EP is termed the exercise price and the exercise cost of purchasing a share via the warrant is:

$$EC = \frac{WP \cdot CR}{n} + EP \qquad (8.3)$$

where:
- EC = exercise cost
- WP = warrant price
- CR = current exchange rate, expressed in units of the equity currency that can be purchased for one unit of the warrant currency. If they are the same currency then $CR = 1$
- EP = exercise price
- n = number of shares that can be purchased per warrant

N.B. in the above the warrant price is the price that has to be paid for the warrant. It is not the market quoted percentage price.

Example ▶

The Mitsui & Co. U.S. dollar warrant of February 1989, gives the holder of a USD 5,000 warrant the right to purchase 565 shares in Mitsui & Co. at a current price of JPY 1138 between 20 February 1989 and 22 January 1993.

If such a warrant is priced at USD 20 per cent the cost of one warrant is 20 x 5000/100 = USD 1000.

The exercise cost (EC) of shares in Mitsui via the warrant would then be:

$$EC = \frac{1000 \times 150}{565} + 1138 \text{ assuming an exchange rate of USD 1 = JPY 150.}$$

$$= 265.5 + 1138 = JPY\ 1403.5\ per\ share$$

The premium/discount of purchasing an equity via a warrant as opposed to purchasing direct is calculated as below:

$$PM = \left\{\frac{EC}{SP} - 1\right\} \cdot 100 \qquad (8.4)$$

where:
- PM = warrant premium/discount %
- EC = exercise cost of purchasing a share via the warrant
- SP = share price

Bond Markets: Structures and Yield Calculations

Example ▸

In the example above, if the equity share price is JPY 1140, then the conversion premium is given by:

$$PM = \left\{\frac{1403.5}{1140} - 1\right\} \times 100 = 23.1\%$$

A warrant has an intrinsic value when the exercise price is less than the share price.

The intrinsic value is given by:

$$IV = (SP - EP) \cdot n \quad \text{if } SP > EP \tag{8.5}$$

where:
- IV = intrinsic value
- SP = share price
- EP = exercise price
- n = number of shares that can be purchased per warrant

For warrants which are expected to be exercised, there is a tendency for the premium or discount to remain stable in the short term, when the share price moves. However, since the warrant price per share is usually considerably less than the share price, the percentage price movement is usually much greater. The effect is known as warrant gearing or leverage and is given by:

$$WG = \frac{SP \cdot n}{WP \cdot CR} \tag{8.6}$$

where:
- WG = warrant gearing
- SP = share price
- WP = warrant price
- CR = current exchange rate, expressed in units of the equity currency that can be purchased for one unit of the warrant currency. If they are the same currency then $CR = 1$
- n = number of shares that can be purchased per warrant

Because of the gearing and the volatility of the value of the underlying asset, warrants are priced at more than their intrinsic value.

8.3 Commodity/currency warrants

Premiums and discounts on commodity and currency warrants may be calculated in the same way as for equity warrants. An example of a currency warrant is given below:

Example ▸

On 26 February 1987 Merrill Lynch issued a currency warrant at USD 50 per warrant which entitles the holder to purchase USD 500 at any time between 3 March 1987 and 15 February 1990 at a fixed exchange rate of DEM 1.815 = USD 1.

CHAPTER 9

MONEY MARKET INSTRUMENTS

Fixed rate money market instruments are generally traded on a discount or yield basis as opposed to a price. However, floating rate instruments (e.g. medium term floating rate certificates of deposit), are quoted on a price basis until there is only one known coupon payment outstanding.

9.1 Discounts

Treasury bills, commercial paper, bankers acceptances etc. are frequently traded on the basis of a discount to par or redemption value. This discount is sometimes referred to as a discount yield and should not be confused with a bond yield.

Discounts are quoted at an annual rate based normally on a 360 or 365-day year in accordance with market convention (e.g. a 365-day year is used for sterling instruments even in a leap year and a 360-day year is used for U.S. dollar ones).

The percentage price paid for a money market instrument quoted at a discount rate R is:

$$P = 100 \cdot \left\{1 - \frac{R \cdot f1}{100}\right\} \tag{9.1}$$

where: P = percentage price
  R = discount rate %
  $f1$ = fraction of a year from settlement to redemption based on actual days divided by the assumed number of days in the year (i.e. 360 or 365)

Example ▶

Consider a bill which will be redeemed on 30 June 1998, and is being traded for settlement on 12 February 1998 at a discount rate of 8.0%. If it were a sterling bill, it would be traded at a percentage price (P) given by:

$$P = 100 \times \left\{1 - \frac{8}{100} \times \frac{138}{365}\right\}$$

$$= 96.9753\% \qquad \text{as there are 138 days between settlement and redemption.}$$

On the other hand if it were a U.S. dollar bill, it would be traded at a percentage price (P) where:

$$P = 100 \times \left\{1 - \frac{8}{100} \times \frac{138}{360}\right\}$$

$$= 96.9333\%$$

Any discount rate can readily be converted into a yield for comparison with other money market instruments. The relationship between them is:

$$MMY = \frac{R}{P} \cdot 100$$

$$MMY = \frac{R}{(1 - R \cdot f1/100)} \tag{9.2}$$

where: MMY = money market yield %
R = discount rate %
P = percentage price
$f1$ = fraction of a year from settlement to redemption

Example ▶

In the above example, the yield on the sterling instrument will be:

$$MMY = 8 / 0.969753 = 8.250\%$$

and for the U.S. dollar instrument:

$$MMY = 8 / 0.969333 = 8.253\%$$

Equation (9.2) above may be re-stated as:

$$MMY = \frac{100 - P}{P \cdot f1}$$

BOND MARKETS: STRUCTURES AND YIELD CALCULATIONS

$$= \frac{100-P}{P} \cdot \frac{a}{d} \qquad (9.3)$$

where d = number of days according to the relevant calendar until redemption.
a = number of days in the calendar year.

This formula is the equivalent of the money market yield formula (5.12) for a security which is redeemed at par.

9.2 Yields

Some money market instruments are quoted on a yield as opposed to a discount basis. One important group of such instruments is fixed rate certificates of deposit (CDs). These are issued at par and accrue interest at a specified rate. The calculation of prices from yields differs according to whether there is one or more further coupon payments. It should be noted that these yields are not the same as the bond yields discussed in chapter 5.

9.2.1 Calculations for instruments with one coupon payment

For a certificate of deposit (CD) or other instrument being traded on a yield basis, with one coupon payment on redemption, the percentage price is given by:

$$P = \frac{(C+k)}{(1 + y \cdot f1)} \qquad (9.4)$$

where:
P = percentage price
C = percentage redemption value (with CDs normally 100%)
k = percentage coupon payment on redemption i.e. $k = g \cdot f$ where g is the quoted annual interest rate and f is the fraction of a year from either the last coupon date or the issue date to redemption
y = quoted yield ($y = 0.08$ for a yield of 8%)
$f1$ = fraction of a year from settlement to redemption

In the above formula the fractions of a year are the actual number of days between the dates divided by the assumed number of days in a days in a year, which is usually 360 or 365-days, depending on the market convention (e.g. for instruments in U.S. dollars it is 360-days, whereas for sterling instruments it is 365-days even in a leap year).

Example ▶

A U.S. dollar CD was issued on 15 August 1997 for redemption on 15 December 1997 with a 9% coupon.

If for settlement on the 16 October 1997 it was trading at 8.4%, the percentage price (P) paid for the CD would have been:

$$P = \frac{(100 + 9 \times 122/360)}{(1 + 0.084 \times 60/360)} = \frac{103.05}{1.014} = 101.627\%$$

On the other hand if it were still trading at 9% the price would have been:

$$P = \frac{(100 + 9 \times 122/360)}{(1 + 0.09 \times 60/360)} = \frac{103.05}{1.015} = 101.527\%$$

9.2.2 Calculation for instruments with more than one coupon

The principle used to calculate the settlement price P of a certificate of deposit (CD) or other money market instrument with more that one future coupon payment, being quoted on a yield basis, is effectively just repeated applications of equation (9.4) for each coupon period in turn allowing for the number of days between each successive coupon date and using simple interest for each period including the first possible part period.

The percentage price of a CD quoted on a yield basis y is given by:

$$P \cdot (1 + y \cdot f1) = \sum_{i=1}^{n} \frac{G_i}{E_i} + \frac{C}{E_n} \qquad (9.5)$$

where:
- P = percentage price of the CD, including any accrued interest
- $f1$ = fraction of a year from the value date to the first/next coupon date i.e. it is the number of days between the two dates divided by the assumed number of days in the year (i.e. 360 or 365)
- y = quoted yield. This yield will be compounded at the same frequency as the coupon payment.
- G_i = ith coupon payment. If the CD has a fixed coupon of $g\%$ p.a. then $G_i = g$ times the number of days since the previous coupon or issue date divided by the assumed number of days in a year
- E_i = aggregate discounting factor for each of the cash flows
- E_1 = 1
- E_i = $E_{i-1} \cdot (1 + y \cdot f_i)$ for $i = 2$ to n
- f_i = fraction of a year of the ith coupon period i.e. number of days divided by the assumed number of days in the year
- n = number of future coupon payments
- C = percentage redemption value

Example ▸

Consider the following U.S. dollar 9% certificate of deposit which pays interest semi-annually on 1 March and 1 September. It will be redeemed on 1 March 1999 at 100%.

BOND MARKETS: STRUCTURES AND YIELD CALCULATIONS

It is being traded for a value date of 1 February 1998 at a yield of 9.25%, having been issued some time ago. What is its price?

The CD has three future coupon payments on 1 March 1998, 1 September 1998 and 1 March 1999. It paid a coupon on 1 September 1997. The three coupon payments are thus $9 \times 181/360$, $9 \times 184/360$ and $9 \times 181/360$ respectively.

Similarly the discounting factors are:

$$E_1 = 1$$
$$E_2 = (1 + 0.0925 \times 184/360) = 1.04728$$
$$E_3 = 1.04728 \times (1 + 0.0925 \times 181/360) = 1.09598$$

Thus the price (P) is given by:

$$P \times (1 + 0.0925 \times 28/360) = \frac{9}{360} \times \left(\frac{181}{1} + \frac{184}{1.04728} + \frac{181}{1.09598}\right) + \frac{100}{1.09598}$$

P = 103.543%

9.3 Floating rate certificates of deposit

Floating rate certificates of deposit (FRCDs) are dealt on a clean price as opposed to a discount or yield basis.

In a similar way to bonds the gross price that has to be paid for a FRCD is given by:

$$P = CP + g \cdot f$$

where:
    P = gross price
    CP = clean price
    g = current coupon rate %
    f = fraction of a year from the last coupon date or issue date to value date. This is measured as actual days divided by 360 or if sterling 365.

N.B. for sterling FRCDs the accrued interest is calculated, unlike Eurosterling FRNs, on the basis of a 365-day year even in a leap year. In other respects FRCDs are evaluated in the same way as FRNs (see chapter 6).

CHAPTER 10

MISCELLANEOUS

10.1 Bonds in default

International bonds in default are governed by ISMA Rule 187.

Rule 187 Bonds in Default.

Where a debtor fails to pay the interest or principal of a bond on the due date such bond must henceforth be traded at a "flat" price and contracts must be marked accordingly. Bonds which are traded at a "flat" price must have all unpaid or partly paid coupons attached.

Other markets often have similar rules. For such bonds any calculations are purely speculative and depend on one's assumptions.

10.2 Tax

Most international securities pay coupons gross, however this is frequently not the case with domestic issues.

It is conventional only to calculate gross yields in Euromarkets, however the formulae can be extended to allow for tax.

There are two main types of tax that may be applied to bond yield calculations, income and capital gains taxes. It is conventional to ignore the timing of any tax payments and assume that they coincide with coupons and capital repayments.

To allow for income tax, if coupon payments are scaled down by the tax rate, the formulae can be applied as normal to produce net yields.

Bond Markets: Structures and Yield Calculations

Example ▶

A bond with an 8% annual coupon is redeemed in 2003 at 100%. It is currently priced at 90%. Coupons are subject to a 25% tax in the hands of the holder, who does not have any capital gains tax liability.

A net after tax coupon of $8 \times (1 - 25/100) = 6\%$ is calculated and put in the yield calculations. However if the bond has not been held for the full period, the tax liability on the first coupon payment may be different.

i.e. an 8% bond subject to 25% income tax is treated as if it were a 6% bond which is not subject to income tax, with the same gross price, and possibly a different first coupon payment.

The standard redemption yield formulae can usually be adapted for capital gains taxes as well. As this tax is frequently applied to the difference between a possibly adjusted purchase price and the selling or redemption price of the security, the normal formulae can be used with the redemption (realization) value reduced by the capital gains tax liability.

Example ▶

If an investor holds a bond until redemption at 100% and is subject to capital gains tax at 25% on the difference between the purchase price of 90% and the redemption price, then his return is identical (subject to possible timing considerations) to holding a bond on which he does not have to pay any capital gains tax which is redeemed on the same date at a price of $(100 - (100 - 90) \times 25/100) = 97.5\%$.

10.3 Prices from yields

It is sometimes desirable to trade a bond on a yield as opposed to a price basis, and then calculate the price/value of the transaction. This is in fact the norm in some domestic markets. This situation may occur in the Euromarkets with new issues before the final terms are fixed.

The formulae used to derive prices are the standard redemption yield ones discussed in chapter 5, however they should only be used in certain situations. Some of the considerations and limitations are listed below:

- the calculation of a price from a yield only applies to fixed rate bonds, including zero coupon bonds. The suggested method cannot be used for floating rate notes or money market instruments.

- for dated bonds, the redemption dates should be agreed/known at the time of the trade.

- for undated (perpetual) bonds, yields are based on the assumption that the bond is never redeemed and the issuer continues to pay coupons at the same rate.

- the quoted yield should unless otherwise agreed at the time of the trade be according to the ISMA formula and compounded annually.

For a dated bond the method of calculating a price from a yield is first to convert the yield to the compounding frequency of the coupon (see Appendix II), and then substitute this yield in the appropriate redemption yield equation to derive a gross price.

Example ▸

The terms for a fixed rate Eurobond are:

- 9% coupon payable semi-annually on 15 January and 15 July
- redeemable at par on 15 July 2005

It is being traded on a yield to maturity (compounded annually) of 10.25% for settlement on 15 March 1990.
This quoted yield is equivalent to a semi-annualized yield of 10.0%, (see Appendix II).

The substitution in equation (5.5) gives:

$$P = v^{0.66667} \times \left\{ 4.5 + 4.5v \times \frac{\left(1 - v^{30}\right)}{(1 - v)} + 100 \times v^{30} \right\}$$

as:
$y = 0.1$
$v = 1/(1 + 0.05) = 0.9238$
$k = 4.5$
$g = 9$
$h = 2$
$f1 = 120/180 = 0.66667$
$f2 = 0$
$C = 100$
$n = 31$

which gives a gross price (including accrued interest):

$P = 93.715\%$

The accrued interest on 15 March is $9 \times 60/360 = 1.5\%$ and hence the clean price is 92.215%.

For undated (perpetual) bonds the method of calculating a price from the yield is first to convert the yield to the compounding frequency of the coupon (see Appendix II) and then substitute the yield in equation (5.15) to derive a gross price.

Example ▶

An undated bond pays a coupon of 10% annually on 15 October. It is being traded on a yield of 8.75% on an annual basis, for settlement on 15 March 1998.

Substituting in equation (5.15) the gross price (P) is given by:

$$P = v^{0.58333} \times (10 + 10/0.0875)$$

as
$$\begin{align} y &= 0.0875 \\ v &= 1/(1 + 0.0875) = 0.91954 \\ k &= 10 \\ g &= 10 \\ h &= 1 \\ f1 &= 210/360 = 0.58333 \end{align}$$

which gives a gross price:

$$P = 118.351\%$$

The accrued interest on 15 March is $10 \times 150/360 = 4.167\%$ and hence the clean price is 114.184%.

CHAPTER 11

BOND MARKET COMPARISONS

This chapter compares the majority of European domestic bond markets, with the expected conventions for the euro market, the international bond market and the major markets elsewhere. Whilst every effort has been made to establish the validity of the data, due, at least in part, to the constantly changing nature of the markets, errors and omissions may have crept in.

It is expected that the bond markets in those countries that adopt the euro, will normally convert government debt to euro at the first appropriate date and adopt the new conventions. It is unclear how much of the non-government debt will be re-denominated into euros. Some debt denominated in legacy currencies may continue to be traded in them, using the existing conventions, throughout their life.

The comparison covers:

- how different types of instruments are normally quoted;
- how much accrued interest, if any, the buyer will have to pay in addition to the traded price;
- the cost of the bond if it is quoted on a yield basis;
- the normal settlement period and where they may be settled;
- the rules for adjusting coupon dates if not fixed;
- the rules for whether the buyer or seller gets the coupon;
- the normal way yields are quoted and calculated together with their compounding frequencies;
- the rates of withholding tax, together with who may reclaim it;
- how the associated money markets accrue interest.

It should be pointed out that although care has been taken to establish the normal trading practices, these are not always followed. In addition, in a few markets, information on some of the less liquid sectors has been omitted.

This comparison covers the next few pages, after which a full guide, covering the terms, abbreviations and footnotes used in the table, is provided.

BOND MARKET COMPARISONS

	Quotation method	Settlement period in days	Accrual basis	Ex-coupon period	Coupon payment frequency and dates	Yield methodology	Yield compounding period	Where settled	Withholding tax (%)	Money market accrual basis
AUSTRALIA										
Government bonds	Y	3	act/365	7	norm.2	RY	bond	AUC,C,E	10	act/365†[1]
AUSTRIA										
Fixed interest	CP%	†[2]	30E/360	†[3]	norm.1	RY	1	C,E,OKB	22†[4]	act/360
BELGIUM										
All except OLO strips	CP%	3	30E/360	none	1	RY-MMY	1	C,E,NBB	15†[5]	act/365
OLO strips	Y	3	30E/360†[6]	none	-	RY-MMY†[7]	1	C,E,NBB	-	
CANADA										
Treasury bills	MMY	Trade date	act/365	-	-	MMY	-	CDS-DCS,C,E	none	act/365†[1]
Government	CP%	2 or 3†[8]	act/365†[9]	none	norm.2	RY-MMY	2	CDS-DCS,C,E	none	
Provincial/Municipal	CP%	3	act/365†[9]	none	norm.2	RY-MMY	2	CDS-BBS,C,E†[10]	none	
Corporate	CP%	3	act/365†[9]	none	norm.2	RY-MMY	2	CDS-BBS,C,E†[10]	0/25†[11]	
CZECH REPUBLIC										
All bonds	CP%	3†[12]	30E/360	30	norm.1	RY	bond	†[13]	0/25†[14]	act/360
DENMARK										
Govt., T-notes, mortgage bonds	CP%	3	30E/360	30	†[15]	RY†[16]	1	VP,C,E	none	act/360
Government FRNs	CP%	3	30E/360	30	4	-†[17]	-	VP,C,E	none	
Zero-coupon T-bills †[18]	P†[19]	3	-	-	-	RY/MMY†[20]	1	VP,C,E	none	
FINLAND										
All bonds	Y	3	30E/360	none	norm.1	RY-MMY	1	C,E,DOM	28†[21]	act/365†[1]

cont.

BOND MARKET COMPARISONS

(cont.)

	Quotation method	Settlement period in days	Accrual basis	Ex-coupon period	Coupon payment frequency and dates	Yield methodology	Yield compounding period	Where settled	Withholding tax (%)	Money market accrual basis
FRANCE										
BTF	MMY	1(Intl.-3)	act/360	none	-	MMY	-	STN‡[22]	none	act/360
BTAN,BMTN,TCN	Y	1(Intl.-3)	act/act	none	1	RY	1	C,E,STN‡[22]	none	
OAT & fixed-rate bonds	CP%	3	act/act	none	1	RY-MMY	1	C,E,SICO,Relit	none	
Post-determined variable bonds	CP%	3	act/year	none	norm.1	-	1	C,E,SICO	none	
Pre-determined FRNs, incl.TEC	CP%	3	act/year	none	norm.4	-	1	C,E,SICO	none	
Convertible bonds	P‡[23]	3‡[24]		none	1	RY	1	SICO‡[25]	none	
GERMANY										
Fixed-rate bonds	CP%	2(Intl.-3)	30E/360	none	norm.1	RY-MMY‡[26]	1	C,E,DC	30‡[27]	act/365
Floating-rate notes	CP%	2(Intl.-3)	act/360	none	norm.2 or 4 - variable ‡[28]		-	C,E,DC	30‡[27]	
GREECE										
FRNs, T-bills, etc. ‡[29]	CP%	2(Intl.-3)	act/365	none	norm.1	-	-	DOM‡[30]	none	act/365
HUNGARY										
Government	CP%	2	act/365‡[31]	1‡[32]	norm.1 or 2	RY-MMY‡[33]	1	Keler RT	0/10‡[34]	act/360
IRELAND										
Government (gilt-edged)										act/365
Fixed-rate - 365-day‡[35]	CP%	1‡[36]	act/365	‡[37]	2	RY	2	C,E,IGSO	none	
Fixed-rate - 360-day‡[35]	CP%	1‡[36]	30E/360	‡[37]	1	RY	2	C,E,IGSO	none	
Fixed-rate - act/act‡[35]	CP%	1‡[36]	act/act	‡[37]	1	RY	2	C,E,IGSO	none	
Variable-rate	CP%	1‡[36]	act/year‡[38]	‡[37]	4	‡[39]	2	C,E,IGSO	none	

cont.

BOND MARKET COMPARISONS

(cont.)

	Quotation method	Settlement period in days	Accrual basis	Ex-coupon period	Coupon payment frequency and dates	Yield methodology	Yield compounding period	Where settled	Withholding tax (%)	Money market accrual basis
ISRAEL										act/year
Government										
*Sagi & Galil	P%	Trade date	act/365	‡40	1	‡41	1	TASE	‡42	
*Kfir	P%	Trade date	act/365	‡40	2	‡43	1	TASE	‡42	
*Gilboa	P%	Trade date	act/365	‡40	2	‡44	1	TASE	‡42	
*Shahar	P%	Trade date	act/365	‡40	1	RY45	1	TASE	none	
*Gilon	P%	Trade date	act/365	4	2	RY‡46	1	TASE	none	
Makam (Treasury bills)	P%									
ITALY										
BOT,CTZ	P%	2‡47	act/365	-	-	MMY	-	C,E,DOM	12.5‡48	act/365‡
Other bonds	CP‡49	3	30E/360‡50	none	norm.2	RY	bond	C,E,DOM	12.5‡51	
JAPAN										
Treasury bills	MMY	2	act/365‡31	-	-	MMY‡52	-	BOJ	18	act/365‡
Government (JGB)	CP%	3	act/365‡31,53	none‡54	2	‡55	-	BOJ	20‡56	
Other bonds	CP%	‡57	act/365‡31	none‡54	norm.2	‡55	-	DOM	20‡56	
LUXEMBOURG										
All bonds	CP%	3	30E/360	none	1	RY-MMY	1	C	none	act/365
NETHERLANDS										
All bonds	CP%	3	30E/360	none	norm.1	RY	1	C,E,Necigef	none	act/360
NEW ZEALAND										
Treasury bills	MMY	2	act/365	-	-	MMY	-	AUC	none	act/365‡
Government bonds	Y	2‡58	act/365	10	norm.2	RY	bond	AUC,C,E	none	

cont.

BOND MARKET COMPARISONS

(cont.)

	Quotation method	Settlement period in days	Accrual basis	Ex-coupon period	Coupon payment frequency and dates	Yield methodology	Yield compounding period	Where settled	Withholding tax (%)	Money market accrual basis
NORWAY										
All bonds	CP%	3	act/365	14	1 or 2‡[60]	RY	1	C,E	none	‡[59]
POLAND										
Fixed-rate notes	CP%	1‡[61]	act/act	5	1	-	1	KDPW	none	
Floating-rate notes	CP%	‡[61]	act/360	10	-	-	-	KDPW		act/365
PORTUGAL										
All bonds	CP%CP‡[62]	4(Intl.-3)	30E/360	none‡[63]	norm.1	RY‡[64]	1	C,E,CVB	20/25‡[65]	act/year
RUSSIA										
Minfin bonds	CP%	7 calendar	30E/360	none‡[66]	1	RY-MMY	1	VN	none	
Federal loan bonds (OFZ)	CP%	Trade date	act/365	-	-	MMY	-	MICEX	-	
Treasury acceptances (GKO)	P%	Trade date	act/360	-	-	MMY	-	MICEX	-	
SLOVAKIA										
Government	CP%	3(Intl.-5)	30E/360‡[67]	7	norm.2	RY	bond	SLOVK		act/360
SPAIN										
All bonds	CP%‡[68]	5‡[69]	act/year	none	norm.1	RY-MMY‡[70]	1	C,E,Expaclear‡[71]	25‡[72]	act/365‡[1]
SWEDEN										
All bonds	Y	3	30E/360	5	norm.1	RY	1	VPC	none	30E/360‡[73]
SWITZERLAND										
Fixed-rate bonds	CP%	3	30E/360‡[74]	none	norm.1	RY	1	SEGA	‡[75]	
Floating-rate notes	CP%	3	act/360	none	norm.2	-	-	SEGA	‡[75]	

cont.

BOND MARKET COMPARISONS

(cont.)

	Quotation method	Settlement period in days	Accrual basis	Ex-coupon period	Coupon payment frequency and dates	Yield methodology	Yield compounding period	Where settled	Withholding tax (%)	Money market accrual basis
TURKEY										
Revenue-sharing certs - A‡[76,77]	P‡[78]	Trade date	act/365	none	norm.1	-	1	TURK	none	act/365
Revenue-sharing certs - B‡[79,77]	P‡[80]	Trade date	act/365	none	norm.1	-	1	TURK	none	
Corporate bonds ‡[81]	Y	Trade date	act/365	none	norm.1	RY	1	ISEC	‡[82]	
FRN-indexed ‡[76]	‡[83]	Trade date‡[84]	act/365	none	norm.1	-	-	ISEC,TURK	none	
Asset-backed securities etc. ‡[85]	MMY	Trade date	act/365	none	-	MMY	-	ISEC	‡[82]	
Treasury bills/FRNs	MMY‡[86,87]	Trade date‡[84]	act/365	none	norm.1	MMY‡[86]	-	ISEC,TURK	none	
Privatization bills - ADM ‡[79]	‡[88]	Trade date	act/365	none	norm.1	MMY	-	TURK	none	
UNITED KINGDOM										
Government (gilt-edged)										act/365
**Fixed-rate*	CP%	1	act/365‡[89]	‡[90]	norm.2	RY	2	CGO,C,E,NSSR	none‡[91]	
**Index-linked*	CP%	1	act/365‡[89]	‡[90]	2	RY‡[92]	2	CGO,C,E	none‡[91]	
**Floating-rate notes*	CP%	1	act/year	‡[90,93]	4.variable‡[28]	-	-	CGO,C,E	none	
**Strips*	Y	1	act/act	-	-	RY	2	CGO,C,E	-	
Bulldogs (foreign)	CP%	1,3 or 5 ‡[94]	30E/360	none	norm.1	RY	1 or 2	CGO,C,E,CREST	none	
Corporate bonds ‡[95]	CP% ‡[96]	5	act/365	‡[97]	norm.2 or 4	RY	2	CREST	25	
UNITED STATES										act/365‡[1]
Treasury bills	D	1	act/360	-	-	MMY	-	Fedwire	-	
Treasury notes & bonds	CP%	1	act/act	none	2	RY-MMY	2	Fedwire	none	
Other bonds	CP%	3	30U/360	none	2	RY-MMY	2	Fedwire	none	

cont.

BOND MARKET COMPARISONS

(cont.)

	Quotation method	Settlement period in days	Accrual basis	Ex-coupon period	Coupon payment frequency and dates	Yield methodology	Yield compounding period	Where settled	Withholding tax (%)	Money market accrual basis
EURO DENOMINATED BONDS‡[98]										
Fixed-rate bonds	CP%	3	act/act‡[99]	-	1 or 2	RY	norm.1	C,E,DOM		act/360
Floating-rate notes	CP%	3	act/360	-	-	-	-	C,E,DOM		‡[100]
INTERNATIONAL BONDS										
Straights & Convertibles	CP%	3	30E/360‡[101,102]	none	norm.1	RY	1	C,E‡[103]	none	
Floating-rate notes	CP%	3	act/360‡[104]	none	norm.2 or 4. variable ‡[28]	-	-	C,E‡[103]	none	

For abbreviations, see accompanying text
‡ - See notes in accompanying text

71

BOND MARKETS: STRUCTURES AND YIELD CALCULATIONS

11.1 Table Headings

The comparative table, uses the following notation in the specified columns. There is a footnote (marked by ‡) where the rules for a specific market sector vary from the norm, or need further qualifications (see section 11.2).

Quotation method

The majority of bonds are quoted as a percentage price, to which accrued interest is added. However, some bonds, e.g. French convertibles, are quoted domestically as an amount per bond while others, e.g. Swedish bonds, are quoted on a yield basis. The conventions may be different if being traded internationally.

The following notation is used:

$CP\%$	clean percentage price, to which accrued interest is added.
$P\%$	gross (dirty) percentage price (i.e. including accrued interest)
CP	clean price per bond, to which accrued interest is added (e.g. Portuguese OTs-Treasury bonds-are quoted per PTE 10,000 bond).
P	actual gross price per bond including any implied accrued interest. (The bond could have a nominal value of, for example, FRF 680).
Y	yield.
MMY	money market yield.
R	discount rate.

Settlement period

In most markets, the normal settlement period is a specified number of business days following the trade date.

Business days obviously differs from market to market. In the Euromarkets, a business day is defined to be a day when the cash market for the currency and Euroclear and Cedel Bank are open. (Euroclear and Cedel Bank only close on 1 January and 25 December).

Other markets settle on either fixed dates, a number of calendar days after the trade date, or the trade date itself. In some markets the normal settlement date is different domestically to internationally.

A number on its own signifies the number of business days after the trade date on which the transaction is normally settled. If the normal international settlement period is different, this is shown in brackets. For example, *4(Intl.-3)* means 4 days domestically and 3 days internationally.

BOND MARKET COMPARISONS

Accrual basis

In most markets interest accrues from the issue date or last coupon date (inclusive) to the settlement date (exclusive), however this is not universally true. For example, in Italy both the coupon and settlement dates are counted. The different methods are described in chapter 3.

The following notation is used in the table:

$$ddd/yyy$$

where   *ddd*   is the day count method. Unless it is specified to the contrary, the day count is from the issuer or last coupon date (inclusive) up to but excluding the value date.

and   *yyy*   is the number of days in the year.

ddd may take the values:

      act   =   actual number of calendar days
      30E   =   30 day month - European style (see chapter 3)
      30U   =   30 day month - U.S. style (see chapter 3).

yyy may take the values:

      360   =   days
      365   =   365 days
      year   =   365 days normally but 366 days in a leap year.
      act   = n times the actual number of days in the period, where n is the number of periods in the year.

For securities with one payment per year, the act/year and act/act methods are normally equivalent.

Ex-coupon period

In some markets (e.g. Denmark, Ireland, Sweden and the U.K.), transactions of securities for settlement just before a coupon date, entitle the seller instead of the buyer, to the coupon, whereas in other markets (e.g. France and the International bond markets) this is not the case.

The rules for when securities start to trade ex the next coupon vary from country to country and sometimes different securities within a country behave differently. In the ex-coupon period accrued interest is normally calculated backwards from the interest payment date to the settlement date.

A number in the column specifies the normal ex-coupon period in calendar days before an interest date.

Bond Markets: Structures and Yield Calculations

Coupon payment frequency and payment dates

In some markets, there is a tradition for bonds to normally have one payment per year (e.g. Belgium and France), whereas in others they normally pay twice a year (e.g. U.K. and U.S.). This in turn has an impact on the normal compounding periodicity for redemption yields.

Coupon payment dates are usually fixed for the life of the bond; however, with most international floating-rate notes the coupon dates vary from year to year according to predefined rules. These rules essentially ensure that a coupon date does not fall on a weekend or a bank holiday.

The rules of how the interest payment dates change are given in a footnote (marked ‡). The absence of a footnote implies that the payment dates are fixed.

Yield calculations

For the majority of fixed rate bonds, redemption yields are calculated according to the ISMA redemption yield formula. However, in some markets for bonds with a life to maturity of less than one year, a money market yield is used.

The main difference between a money market yield and the ISMA redemption yield calculation is that the money market yield uses simple interest, whereas the redemption yield uses compound interest. It can be seen that the two are, in fact, identical for a bond with an annual coupon with exactly one year to redemption, assuming the yield compounding period is one year.

The ISMA redemption yield and the money market yield formulae are described in chapters 5 and 9. In particular, equation (5.3) is the general redemption yield formula, and equations (5.12) and (9.3) the money market yield formulae.

The following notation is used in the table:

RY	-	ISMA redemption yield throughout the life of the security.
$RY - MMY$	-	ISMA redemption yield until the last coupon period, when a money market yield is used.
MMY	-	Money market yield.

In the majority of European markets, redemption yields are quoted with the interest being compounded annually, whereas in the U.K. and U.S. they are quoted with a semi-annual compounding period. This difference reflects the normal coupon payment frequency in the markets. It is easy to convert a yield with one compounding frequency to another. (See Appendix II).

In some markets, the yields on bonds are compounded with the frequency of the bond's coupon payments. This means that yields cannot always be easily compared

Bond Market Comparisons

between two bonds. The word 'bond' signifies this in the compounding frequency column.

Where settled

The majority of European bonds tend to be settled on a domestic system. However, increasingly, they can also be settled on one of the International clearing houses, Cedel Bank and Euroclear.

The following abbreviations are used:

AUC	=	Austraclear
BOJ	=	Bank of Japan
C	=	Cedel Bank
CDS-BBS	=	Canadian Depository for Securities - Book based system
CDS-DCS	=	Canadian Depository for Securities - Debt clearing system
CGO	=	U.K. Central Gilt Office
CREST	=	U.K. Crest System
CVB	=	Central de Valores Mobiliarios
DC	=	Deutsche Börse Clearing (formerly the Deutscher Kassenverein)
DOM	=	Domestic
E	=	Euroclear
IGSO	=	Irish Gilt Settlement Office operated by the Central Bank of Ireland
ISEC	=	Istanbul Stock Exchange Clearing & Settlement Bank
KDPW	=	Polish Domestic Clearing House
NBB	=	National Bank of Belgium
NSSR	=	National Savings Stock Register
OKB	=	Oesterreichische Kontrollbank
SEGA	=	Swiss Securities Clearing Corporation
SICO	=	Sicovam
SLOVK	=	Slovakian Securities Centre
STN	=	Saturne
TASE	=	Israeli domestic clearing house
TURK	=	Central Bank of Turkey
VN	=	Russian Vneschtorbank
VP	=	Danish Securities Centre (Vaerdipapircentralen)

Withholding tax

In some markets bond coupons are distributed after withholding tax has been deducted, whereas in others this is not the case. The standard rate of withholding tax is frequently specified, together with a note on who may reclaim the tax.

BOND MARKETS: STRUCTURES AND YIELD CALCULATIONS

Money market interest accrual basis

It is important to consider how bond markets and the associated money markets work together. This is especially true with the development of the repo and swap markets, where the final consideration is dependent on both money market interest and bond coupon accrual rates and conventions.

The money markets often have different rules to the bond markets for accruing interest. In some currencies, even the domestic and international money markets have different conventions (e.g. Canadian dollars and Japanese yen accrue interest with a year of 365-days domestically, but with a year of 360-days in Europe).

The notation used in the table is the same as for the coupon interest accrual.

Other abbreviations used

BOT	*Buoni Ordinari del Tesoro*
BMTN	*Bons à Moyen Terme Negociables*
BTAN	*Bons du Trésor à interêt Annuel*
BTF	*Bons du Trésor à Taux Fixe*
CTZ	*Certificati del Tesoro - Zero Coupon*
DIBOR	Dublin interbank offer rate
FRN	Floating-rate note
JGB	Japanese Government Bond
LIBOR	London interbank offer rate
OAT	*Obligations Assimilables du Trésor*
OLO	*Obligation Linéaire - lineaire obligatie*
OT	*Obrigações do Tesouro*
OTC	Over the counter market
TCN	*Titres de Créance Negociables*
TEC	*Taux de l'Echéance Constante*

11.2 Footnotes (‡)

1. Accrues on an actual/365-day basis domestically, but on an actual/360-day basis on the Euromarkets.

2. AT The first banking business day of the second week after the trade date. This rule will be changed in the near future to trade date + 5 business days (T+5) and, later on, to trade date + 3 business days (T+3).

3. AT When the coupon date is between the 10th and 24th of the month, then the ex-coupon date is the first Monday of the same month. When the coupon date is between the 25th of the ongoing month and the 9th of the following month, the ex-coupon date is the third Monday of the ongoing month.

BOND MARKET COMPARISONS

4.   AT   Foreigners not resident in Austria, and companies, are not subject to the withholding tax.

5.   BE   Belgian residents receive payments after a withholding tax of 15%. There is no withholding tax for non-residents and certain exempt organisations such as Credit Institutions.

6.   BE   The accrual basis is actual/365 (the money market convention) when the strip has a life of less than one year.

7.   BE   OLO (*Obligation linéaire - lineaire obligatie*) strips have a price calculated from an ISMA yield (on a 30E/360-day basis) if their life to maturity is greater than one year. For strips with a life of less than one year, a price based on a money market yield using an actual/365 day year is calculated.

8.   CA   Bonds with a life to maturity of over 3 years settle after 3 days. Shorter bonds settle after 2 days.

9.   CA   The Investment Dealer Association (IDA) rule 800.35 states:

   Where interest on a transaction involves an amount greater than that represented by the half-yearly coupon, interest is to be calculated on the basis of the full amount of coupon less one or two days, as the case may be.

Example ▸

If a bond pays a coupon on 15 May and 15 November, where there are 184 days between 15 May and 15 November.

The number of days accrued on the following dates are:

12 November	*181 days*
13 November	*182 days - unchanged*
14 November	*183 days - adjusted to 182½-1 = 181½ days*
15 November	*0 days - coupon date*

---

10. CA   It is planned that eventually all Canadian securities will be cleared domestically through the DCS system

11. CA   Certain long term debt has 0% withholding tax. Others have 25%.

12. CZ   There is no normal period in the OTC market.

BOND MARKETS: STRUCTURES AND YIELD CALCULATIONS

13. CZ   Bonds can be settled on the Prague Stock Exchange, the Securities Central Registry and the RM-System.
Treasury bills settle in the TKD System, which is run by the Czech National Bank.

14. CZ   Government bonds are tax-free. Bonds issued by banks, municipalities and companies are subject to taxation at 25%. This may be reclaimed by foreign residents of countries which have double taxation agreements with the Czech Republic.

15. DK   Usually 1 for Government bonds and Treasury notes, and 2 or 4 for Mortgage Bonds.

16. DK   On mortgage bonds, which are issued over a period of time, the exact cash flows used in the yield calculations are calculated and published by the issuer. During the issuing period, a synthetic profile is projected on the anticipated final amount of the issue.

    For index-linked bonds, the calculations disregard the inflation index element resulting in real-interest yields.

17. DK   The coupon rate is computed from the average yield r on government fixed-rate notes and bonds with a remaining life of more than three months, and less than three years. The average yield is calculated from a period running from 6 months and 10 days before the coupon-date to 3 months and 10 days before the coupon-date. Since all fixed-rate government issues pay coupons annually, the coupon rate C on FRN's is :

$$C = \left\{(1 + r)^{0.25} - 1\right\} \cdot 100$$

18. DK   *Skatkammerbeviser*

    They are usually issued with a life of 3, 6 or 9 months.

19. DK   The actual price is for an amount of DKK 1,000,000.

20. DK   Yields are calculated according to both money market and bond market conventions.

    The official conversion from price to yield, and vice versa, takes place according to money market practice. Using this convention, the yield is given by:

$$\text{Money market yield} = \frac{1,000,000 - Price}{Price} \cdot \frac{360}{d}$$

    where d = actual number of calendar days remaining.

For the same security a bond yield may also be calculated.

It is given by:

$$\text{Bond yield} = \left\{ 1 + \frac{1,000,000 - \text{Price}}{\text{Price}} \right\}^{360/db} - 1$$

where db = number of bond days (on a 360E basis) to maturity.

21. FI Only for domestic private investors.

22. FR BTFs and BTANs will be settled on RGV/Relit from mid 1997.

23. FR Internationally, French Convertible issues are sometimes traded on a percentage price basis.

24. FR A few convertible issues are quoted on the 'monthly settlement' market as equities.

25. FR It is possible to settle these through Euroclear and Cedel Bank.

26. DE Although the ISMA method of calculating yields is most commonly used, it should be noted that some domestic institutional investors and savings banks prefer the Braess/Fangmeyer or Moosmüller methods. Both these methods discount the interest in any fractional period on a simple interest, rather than a compound interest, basis. For bonds with annual coupon payments, the two methods are equivalent.

27. DE Foreign investors are not subject to withholding tax. Some residents (e.g. foundations) may reclaim all, or part, of the withholding tax.

28. The interest payment dates on floating-rate notes are not fixed dates, but are usually determined as described in chapter 2.

    Interest dates for Euro-French Franc floating-rate notes are usually the third Wednesday of the third month of each quarter. (MATIF settlement date).

29. GR Includes foreign currency indexed bonds. There are currently no fixed rate drachma bonds, although some are expected in the not too distant future.

30. GR In the domestic market, securities may be in physical or book-entry form. Book-entry securities are settled through the Bank of Greece. It is planned for all domestic securities to be only in book-entry form and for settlement to be also possible through Cedel Bank and Euroclear.

31. Actual days ignoring leap days (29 February) divided by 365. i.e. there are 2 days between 27 February and 1 March, even in a leap year.

BOND MARKETS: STRUCTURES AND YIELD CALCULATIONS

32. HU   Applies to OTC trades.

33. HU   The money market yield applies whenever the maturity is within 365 days.

34. HU   The 10% withholding tax only applies to private individuals when they do not buy through a broker/dealer firm.

35. IE   Irish government (gilt-edged) fixed-rate stocks issued before 14 June 1993 accrue interest on a 365-day year and have two coupons per year. Stocks issued between June 1993 and August 1997 accrue interest on a 360-day year with one coupon per year, and from September 1997 on an actual/actual day basis.

36. IE   Traditionally, settlement was for 'cash' i.e. next business day. It is now common to have settlement from anywhere between one and five business days.

37. IE   Stocks normally trade ex-coupon from the nearest Wednesday which is three weeks before each coupon date. The actual schedule is issued annually by the Central Bank of Ireland. (For 1996, it was issued in July 95).

38. IE   The coupon rate for each stock is declared by the authorities two days before the start of the coupon period to which the rate will apply: i.e. two days before the coupon date for the previous period. The coupon rate is based on the average DIBOR over the preceding 10 business days, plus or minus a margin associated with the particular stock. The margin currently ranges from -0.04 to +0.04 for different stocks. This rate is then divided by four to give the quarterly coupon rate.

39. IE   The redemption yield is sometimes calculated with the assumption that the coupon rate remains fixed for the rest of the bond's life. It is more usual to treat these bonds as 3-month money market instruments and to calculate a simple interest rate.

40. IL   Usually 2 weeks.

41. IL   The *Sagi* and *Galil* are CPI (consumer price index) linked bonds with a fixed coupon of 4%. The *Sagi* is issued with a maturity of 6 years and the *Galil* with 15 years.

The price is given by:

$$P = \left\{ \sum_{i=1}^{n} g \cdot v^{f1+i-1} + C \cdot v^{f1+n-1} \right\} \cdot \frac{M1}{M0}$$

where P = bond price
g = annual coupon rate %
n = number of coupon payments to redemption
$f1$ = fraction of a period from value date to the first/next interest payment
C = redemption value (= 100)
$M0$ = base CPI
$M1$ = known CPI
v = discounting factor i.e. $v = 1/(1+y)$
y = redemption yield. ($y = 0.08$ for a yield of 8%).

42. IL Tax rates vary according to the status of the investors. Israeli investors pay a maximum tax of 35% on coupon payments. (This applies to private individuals, companies and mutual funds). On the other hand, non-profit organisations - including pension funds and provident funds - are exempt from tax for the holding period.

    Foreign investors usually pay 25% tax, but this depends on the double taxation treaty agreement.

43. IL The *Kfir* is a CPI-linked bond which is issued with a maturity of 7 years. The interest is variable and determined semi-annually according to the average yield-to-maturity on CPI-linked government bonds with a maturity of 3-5 years.

    The price P is given by:

$$P = v^{f1} \cdot \left\{ k^* + \sum_{i=2}^{n} g^* \cdot v^{0.5(i-1)} + 100 \cdot v^{0.5(n-1)} \right\} \cdot \frac{M1}{M0}$$

where: P = bond price
k^* = next known semi-annual coupon
$k^* = \left\{(1 + k/100)^{0.5} - 1\right\} \cdot 100$
k = next known annual coupon
g^* = the forecast semi-annual coupon
$g^* = \left\{(1 + g/100)^{0.5} - 1\right\} \cdot 100$
g = variable interest rate as published by the Bank of Israel
$M0$ = base CPI
$M1$ = known CPI
n = number of coupon payments to redemption
$f1$ = fraction of a year from the value date to the first/next interest payment
v = discounting factor i.e. $v = 1/(1+y)$
y = redemption yield. ($y = 0.08$ for a yield of 8%).

BOND MARKETS: STRUCTURES AND YIELD CALCULATIONS

44.   IL   The *Gilboa* is a government bond linked to the U.S. dollar with a maturity of five years. The coupon rate is set to (LIBOR - 0.25%).

The price P is given by:

$$P = v^{f1} \cdot \left\{ k + \sum_{i=2}^{n} \frac{g \cdot v^{0.5(i-1)}}{2} + 100 \cdot v^{0.5(n-1)} \right\} \cdot \frac{M1}{M0}$$

where:
P = bond price
k = known next semi-annual coupon payment
g = expected subsequent coupon payments, based on the current value of LIBOR
$M0$ = base U.S. dollar rate
$M1$ = known U.S. dollar rate, adjusted for forecast monthly devaluation rate
n = number of coupon payments to redemption
$f1$ = fraction of a year from the value date to the first/next interest payment
v = discounting factor i.e. $v = 1/(1+y)$
y = redemption yield. ($y = 0.08$ for a yield of 8%).

45.   IL   The *Gilon* is an unlinked variable-rate bond, with the interest being based on the weighted average yield of *Makam* (Treasury bills) with maturities of between 3-12 months, plus a fixed premium.
The price P is given by:

$$P = v^{f1} \cdot \left\{ k^* + \sum_{i=2}^{n} g^* \cdot v^{0.5(i-1)} + 100 \cdot v^{0.5(n-1)} \right\}$$

where
P = bond price
k^* = next known semi-annual coupon
$k^* = \left\{ (1 + k/100)^{0.5} - 1 \right\} \cdot 100$
k = next known annual coupon
g^* = assumed subsequent semi-annual coupon
This is based on the variable *Makam* interest rate as published by the Bank of Israel and the fixed premium.
n = number of coupon payments to redemption
$f1$ = fraction of a year from the value date to the first/next interest payment
v = discounting factor i.e. $v = 1/(1+y)$
y = redemption yield. ($y = 0.08$ for a yield of 8%).

46.   IL   A bond redemption yield is used, not a money market yield, based on a 365-day year.

47.   IT   CTZ's settle on trade date plus 3 business days.

BOND MARKET COMPARISONS

48. IT The withholding tax is based on the difference between the issue price and par. BOT's and CTZ's issued after January 1997 will not be subject to withholding tax, nor will existing CTZ's maturing in 1998 or later.

49. IT Bonds are currently traded with the *net* accrued interest added to the price. This will change after the bond's first coupon payment in 1997 to the gross accrued interest being added.

50. IT The number of days accrued includes both the last coupon date and the settlement date. i.e. it is one more day than the norm.

51. IT Currently coupons on newly issued securities are subject to a withholding tax of 12.5%. However, for older issues, this rate could be 0%, 6.25% or 10.0%.

    There is no withholding tax on Italian domestic securities for non-residents in countries with double taxation agreements, and residents subject to corporation tax.

    The withholding tax is based on the coupons paid and the difference between the issue price and the redemption price.

52. JP The Japanese Ministry of Finance announces a yield that is based on a number of days which counts both the issue date and the maturity date.

53. JP Prior to the first coupon payment date, the issue date and the settlement date are included in the number of days accrued.

54. JP Japanese bonds have periods when they cannot be traded. For JGBs, the last trading day is eight business days ahead of the coupon payment day, and for non-JGBs the 'lock up' period is three weeks.

55. JP Frequently quote a simple yield to maturity - see chapter 5.

56. JP For non-exempt Japanese domestic corporations and individuals.

57. JP Usually settled on the 10th, 20th and last day of each month. If this is not a business day, the following business day is used. It is proposed to change this to T+7 in December 1997.

58. NZ Internationally 7 calendar days.

59. NO Money markets accrue interest on a variety of methods. (i.e. 30E/360, actual/360, actual/365 and actual/actual).

BOND MARKETS: STRUCTURES AND YIELD CALCULATIONS

60. NO Some floating rate notes have four coupons a year. These often have coupon dates that vary in the same way as international floating rate notes.

61. PL In the secondary block market, settlement is after two days. In the public market, it is after three days.

    In the primary market two-year notes are settled on the 5th day of the next month after the auction. Five-year notes are settled on the 12th day of the next month after the auction.

    Fixed-rate notes are not traded internationally.

62. PT Treasury bonds - OTs (*Obrigçaões do Tesouro*) are priced domestically as a price per bond, to which accrued interest has to be added.

63. PT Treasury bonds (OTs) cannot be traded for four business days before the coupon payment dates.

64. PT Yields are compounded with the fractional period being calculated as actual days/365, although bonds accrue interest on a 30E/360-day basis.

65. PT Most bonds are subject to 20% withholding tax, although some OT's have coupons paid gross. Corporate euro-escudo bonds have a withholding tax of 25% if there is no paying agent in Portugal. The withholding tax may be reclaimed by non-residents, if there is a suitable double taxation agreement, and some tax free domestic institutions.

66. RU Not tradable in the 30 days before a coupon date.

67. SK Calculated to the trade date, not the settlement date.

68. ES Government bonds do not accrue interest until the first normal coupon date with the result that the first coupon payment is a full one. The period before the first normal coupon payment, during which the bond is effectively priced gross ($P\%$) can be several months.

69. ES A reduction to 3 business days is being considered.

70. ES The yields are compounded with fractional periods being calculated as actual days/365, although bonds accrue interest on an actual/actual basis.

71. ES Government bonds and Public Debt (*Deuda Publica Española*) can be only settled on Euroclear and Cedel. Private debt and Matadors (Peseta Foreign Bonds) can settle on Expaclear as well.

BOND MARKET COMPARISONS

72.	ES	Foreign investors, who are not in tax havens, may reclaim the withholding tax.
73.	CH	For money market instruments in securities form (European Commercial Paper-ECP) the rules of the Euromarket apply. i.e. interest accrues on an actual/360 day basis.
74.	CH	The accrued interest is calculated from the last coupon date before the trade date (not before the settlement date).

Example ▶

For a bond with:

- annual coupon date   30 August
- trade date   28 August 1995
- settlement date   4 September 1995

the number of days accrued interest is 364 (which means that the amount of accrued is larger than the coupon amount). On the other hand, the bond is delivered with the coupon due 30 August 1995.

75.	CH	For non-Swiss issuers, there is no withholding tax. For domestic issuers, there is a withholding tax of 35%. Depending on the domicile of the holder any withholding tax may be partially, or completely, reclaimed.
76.	TR	Indexed to foreign exchange or wholesale prices.
77.	TR	These securities are issued by the Privatisation Administration, a governmental body which conducts privatisation operations. They are hardly marketable. Banks buy them for their reserve requirements at the Central Bank of Turkey and construction companies hold them against public debt.
78.	TR	These instruments are not traded in the secondary market. Hence there is no accepted pricing method.
79.	TR	Indexed to foreign currency.
80.	TR	The price P is given by:

$$P = \frac{(1 + ERP) \cdot R}{1 + (LIBOR + S) \cdot DTM/36500}$$

BOND MARKETS: STRUCTURES AND YIELD CALCULATIONS

> where:
> R = Central Bank of Turkey foreign currency buying rate
> S = spread over LIBOR
> DTM = days to maturity or next coupon date
> ERP = expected next revenue payment

81. TR — Corporate bonds are issued mainly by family-owned enterprises. The secondary market is provided by banks or brokerage houses which underwrite the issue. This has a negative effect on the pricing.

82. TR — 11% for publicly open companies. Otherwise, 22%.

83. TR — No standard method exists, as not actively traded.

84. TR — Domestically, trade date. Internationally, trade date plus two business days.

85. TR — Asset backed securities, commercial paper, and bank bills.

86. TR — FRNs are priced as if they were redeemed on the first coupon date.

87. TR — A money market yield is used in the organised bond market on the Istanbul Stock Exchange. On the other hand, the Central Bank of Turkey uses the following convention for the reserve requirement calculations.

$$Price = Nominal\,(100{,}000) + Coupon \cdot f1$$

> where: $f1$ = the fraction of a period from the last coupon date to the value date.

88. TR — The price P is given by:

$$P = \frac{1}{1 + (LIBOR + S) \cdot d/36500} \cdot R$$

> where:
> R = Central Bank of Turkey foreign currency buying rate
> S = margin over LIBOR
> d = number of days to maturity

89. GB — The accrual basis will change to actual/actual days in the period during 1998.

90. GB — The ex-coupon period is 7 business days with the exception of War Loan where it is 10 days.

BOND MARKET COMPARISONS

91. GB   From 6 April 1998, all gilt interest will be payable without deduction of withholding tax.

92. GB   A 'real' rate of return after assuming an inflation rate is calculated - see Appendix III.

93. GB   The Treasury Floating Rate 2001, which can only be settled in the CGO does not go ex-coupon.

94. GB   The normal settlement period for a bulldog bond is dependent on where the bonds are held and in what form (i.e. registered or bearer).

- If the bonds are held on the Central Gilts Office (CGO) register, then the normal settlement period is 1 day.

- If they are held in registered form, settlement is through Crest after five days.

- If, on the other hand, they are held in bearer form, then they will normally be settled at Cedel Bank or Euroclear after three days.

95. GB   This market still retains many anomalies and exceptions to the following rules.

96. GB   Convertible bonds are sometimes traded on a gross (dirty) price basis *P%*.

97. GB   Some, but not all corporate bonds are traded ex-coupon. The period during which they are traded ex-coupon varies from bond to bond.

98. EU   Anticipated rules.

99. EU   Some debt issued originally in European Currency Units (XEU), which will be automatically converted to euro (EUR), may continue to trade using the existing conventions.

100.   In the international markets, interest is normally calculated on an actual/360-day basis. However some currencies calculate interest on an actual/365-day basis and some even have two standards. Japanese Yen (JPY) and Canadian Dollars (CAD) are examples of currencies with two standards. e.g. Japanese yen lent in Japan would calculate on an actual/365-day basis, but Japanese yen lent in Europe (euroyen) would calculate on an actual/360-day basis.

Currencies which accrue on an actual/365-day basis include Belgian francs, domestic Canadian dollars, Irish pounds, Italian lire, domestic Japanese yen, sterling and domestic U.S. dollars.

BOND MARKETS: STRUCTURES AND YIELD CALCULATIONS

101.   The market practice is for Canadian dollar global bonds to behave normally as domestic Canadian dollar bonds, unless the prospectus says otherwise. i.e. they accrue interest on an actual/365-day basis.

102.   It is proposed that all new international bonds issued after 1 January 1999 will accrue interest on an actual/actual basis, regardless of whether the European single currency is introduced on that date.

103.   It is also possible to settle euro French franc bonds on Sicovam.

104.   Eurosterling and Irish pound bonds accrue interest on an actual/365-day basis as opposed to actual/360.

APPENDIX I

THE GENERAL REDEMPTION YIELD FORMULA

The redemption yield y of a security, compounded annually, is given by solving an equation of the form:

$$P = \sum_{i=1}^{n} CF_i \cdot v^{L_i}$$

where:
- P = gross price (i.e. clean price plus accrued interest)
- n = number of future cash flows, where n may be infinite
- CF_i = ith cash flow
- L_i = time in years to the ith cash flow, taking into account the market conventions for calculating the fraction of a year. (e.g. does the year have 360 or 365-days).
- v = discounting factor i.e. $v = 1/(1 + y)$
- y = required redemption yield compounded annually ($y = 0.08$ for a yield of 8%).

This general redemption yield formula, which assumes that all cash flows irrespective of their timing are discounted at the same rate, works for all securities. In the case of partly paid issues, future price calls are regarded as negative cash flows. Similarly for undated bonds n is infinite, as it is assumed that the issuer never defaults.

In chapter 4 we stated that the modified duration MD of a bond was given by:

$$MD = -\frac{dP}{dy} \cdot \frac{1}{P}$$

where:
- P = gross price (i.e. clean price plus accrued interest)
- dp = small change in price
- dy = corresponding small change in yield

From the redemption yield formula above we have:

$$\frac{dP}{dy} = \frac{dP}{dv} \cdot \frac{dv}{dy} = \left(\sum_{i=1}^{n} CF_i \cdot L_i \cdot v^{L_i - 1}\right) \cdot \left\{\frac{-1}{(1+y)^2}\right\}$$

Hence:

$$MD = \frac{1}{P} \cdot \sum_{i=1}^{n} CF_i \cdot L_i \cdot v^{L_i + 1}$$

On the other hand, the duration D (equation 4.4) is just:

$$D = \frac{1}{P} \cdot \sum_{i=1}^{n} CF_i \cdot L_i \cdot v^{L_i}$$

thus:

$$MD = D \cdot v$$

which is equation (4.8).

Similarly convexity CX is defined in chapter 4 to be:

$$CX = \frac{1}{P} \cdot \frac{d^2 P}{dy^2} = \frac{1}{P} \cdot \frac{d}{dy}\left(\frac{dP}{dy}\right)$$

$$= \frac{1}{P} \cdot \sum_{i=1}^{n} CF_i \cdot L_i \cdot (L_i + 1) \cdot v^{L_i + 2}$$

The redemption yield formula can be solved in a general way using the Newton-Raphson method.

$$\text{Let } f(v) = P - \sum_{i=1}^{n} CF_i \cdot v^{L_i}$$

then the first derivative $df/dv = f^1(v)$ is given by:

$$f^1(v) = -\sum_{i=1}^{n} L_i \cdot CF_i \cdot v^{L_i - 1}$$

We want to establish a value of v which is a root of $f(v)$. (i.e. $f(v)=0$). This value then defines the required redemption yield y.

APPENDIX I – THE GENERAL REDEMPTION YIELD FORMULA

The method uses an iterative process for solving the equation. The process is started by estimating a discounting value v_0. A better estimate v_1 is then given by:

$$v_1 = v_0 - f(v_0)/f^1(v_0)$$

This process is then repeated as often as necessary. i.e.

$$v_{i+1} = v_i - f(v_i)/f^1(v_i)$$

until the change in v from one iteration to the next is within the required accuracy. Assuming that $i=m$ when this is achieved, the required redemption yield y compounded annually is given by:

$$v_m = 1/(1 + y)$$

or $$y = (1 - v_m)/v_m$$

Similarly the duration D is:

$$D = - \frac{1}{P} \cdot f^1(v_m) \cdot v_m$$

An initial approximation which is reasonable in most circumstances is:

$$y_o = \frac{\sum_{i=1}^{n} CF_i - P}{\sum_{i=1}^{n} L_i \cdot CF_i}$$

where: $$v_0 = 1/(1 + y_0)$$

APPENDIX II

COMPOUNDING FREQUENCY ADJUSTMENTS

The normal redemption yield formulae described produce yields that are compounded with the periodicity of the coupon payments. For zero-coupon bonds, this is normally assumed to be the same as for the compounding frequency of the market.

A redemption yield which is compounded annually can be converted to a semi-annual compounding yield, and vice versa, very easily - irrespective of the coupon frequency.

Redemption yields with different compounding frequencies are related by the formulae:

$$(1 + y_a) = \left(1 + \frac{y_s}{2}\right)^2 = \left(1 + \frac{y_q}{4}\right)^4 = \left(1 + \frac{y_m}{12}\right)^{12}$$

where: y_a = yield compounded annually
y_s = yield compounded semi-annually
y_q = yield compounded quarterly
y_m = yield compounded monthly

In the above formulae, yields of 12% would be substituted as 0.12 etc.

If it is required to convert a yield with a compounding frequency of h times per year to one with a compounding frequency of r times per year, the equation may be restated as:

$$y_r = r \cdot \left\{\left(1 + \frac{y_h}{h}\right)^{h/r} - 1\right\}$$

APPENDIX II – COMPOUNDING FREQUENCY ADJUSTMENTS

where: y_r = yield compounded r times per year
y_h = yield compounded h times per year
r = required compounding frequency per year
h = original compounding frequency per year

Example ▶

If a bond has a yield (y_q) compounded quarterly of 10% then it will have yields compounded semi-annually (y_s) and annually (y_a) given by:

$$y_s = 2 \times \left(1 + \frac{y_q}{4}\right)^2 - 2$$

$$= 2 \times (1.025)^2 - 2$$

$$= 0.10125 = 10.125\%$$

$$y_a = \left(1 + \frac{y_q}{4}\right)^4 - 1$$

$$= (1.025)^4 - 1$$

$$= 0.10381 = 10.381\%$$

Example ▶

If a bond has an annually compounded yield (y_a) of 8%, then its semi-annually compounded yield (y_s) is given by:

$$y_s = 2 \times \left\{(1 + y_a)^{0.5} - 1\right\}$$

$$= 2 \times \left\{1.08^{0.5} - 1\right\} = 0.07846 = 7.846\%$$

APPENDIX III

INDEX-LINKED STOCKS AND REAL RETURNS

In some markets, stocks have been issued where the coupons and final redemption value are linked to a measure of purchasing power or inflation. An example of such stocks are the British index-linked gilt-edged securities where the coupon and redemption values are linked to the U.K. Retail Price Index, albeit lagged by 8 months.

For such stocks it is conventional to calculate a 'real' redemption yield which discounts the effect of any rise in the index, and the corresponding increase in the payments.

For index-linked stocks, it is normal for the first payment to be known, and for there to be a lag between the index reference date and the indexed payment dates.

For a stock which pays an indexed coupon h times a year, with a similarly indexed redemption value the general redemption yield formula:

$$P = \sum_{i=1}^{n} CF_i \cdot v^{L_i}$$

where:
- P = gross price (i.e. clean price plus accrued interest)
- n = number of future cash flows
- CF_i = ith cash flow, which changes with the underlying index.
- L_i = time in years to the ith cash flow
- v = the gross discounting factor, i.e. $v = 1/(1+y/h)$
- h = number of periods in year
- y = the required redemption yield compounded h times per annum. ($y = 0.08$ for a yield of 8%)

can be restated as follows.

APPENDIX III – INDEX-LINKED STOCKS AND REAL RETURNS

If the assumed rate of indexing is $r\%$ per period, the next known coupon payment is k, and the best estimate of the following coupon is k_2, then it is assumed that the ith coupon payment is:

$$k_2 \cdot (1 + r)^{i-2} \text{ for } i \geq 2$$

It should be noted that it is often possible to make a better estimate of k_2 than $k \cdot (1 + r)$, since the index value for at least part of the period is already known due to the lagging.

Similarly the assumed redemption value is estimated as:

$$C \cdot (1 + r)^{n-2}$$

where C is the redemption value if the index was the same as for k_2

The real rate of return y is given by solving:

$$P = v^{f1} \cdot \left\{ k + \sum_{i=2}^{n} k_2 \cdot (1 + r)^{i-2} \cdot v^{i-1} + C \cdot (1 + r)^{n-2} \cdot v^{n-1} \right\}$$

where:
- C = redemption value calculated at the same index level as the next coupon payment k
- k = next known coupon payment
- k_2 = best estimate of the subsequent coupon payment.
- $f1$ = fraction of a period from value date to the first/next coupon payment. A period is defined as the normal time between two consecutive coupon payments
- v = overall discounting factor, i.e.

$$v = \frac{1}{(1 + r) \cdot (1 + y/h)}$$

- r = assumed indexing rate per period
- h = number of coupon payments per year
- y = real rate of return per year (i.e. $y = 0.04$ for a real return of 4.0%).

This formula may be restated as:

$$P = \left\{ \frac{w}{1+r} \right\}^{f1} \cdot \left\{ k + \frac{w}{1+r} \cdot \left(\sum_{i=2}^{n} k_2 \cdot w^{i-2} + C \cdot w^{n-2} \right) \right\}$$

where: w = 'real' discounting factor, i.e.
$w = 1/(1+y/h) = v \cdot (1 + r)$

BOND MARKETS: STRUCTURES AND YIELD CALCULATIONS

In the U.K., the Retail Price Index used in the calculations reflects the index value two months before the start of the coupon period, i.e. 8 months before the actual payment, as they all have two payments per year.